THEATRICAL STYLE

A Visual Approach to the Theatre

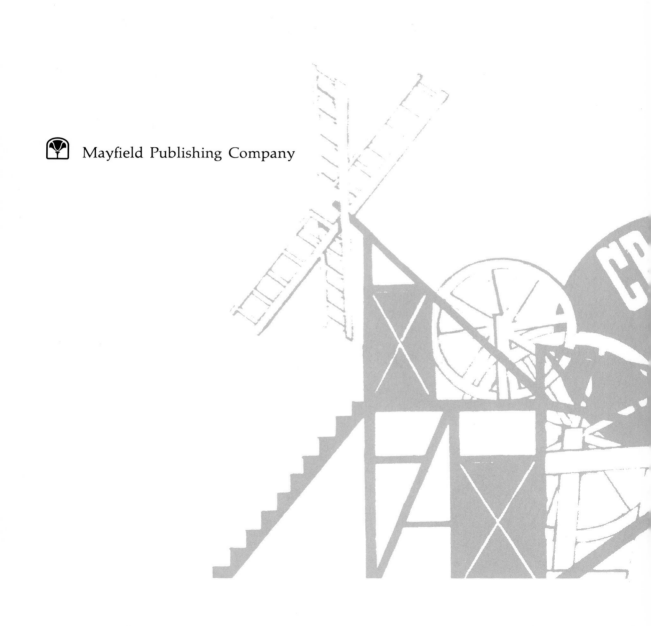

Mayfield Publishing Company

THEATRICAL STYLE

A Visual Approach to the Theatre

DOUGLAS A. RUSSELL
Stanford University

To Norman Philbrick

Library of Congress Catalog Card Number: 75-21072
International Standard Book Number: 0-87484-226-3

Manufactured in the United States of America
Mayfield Publishing Company
285 Hamilton Avenue, Palo Alto, California 94301

This book was set in Elegante by Applied Typographic
Systems and was printed and bound by National Press.
Sponsoring editor was C. Lansing Hays, Carole Norton
supervised editing, and Marjorie Cutler was manuscript
editor. Michelle Hogan supervised production, and the
book was designed by Nancy Sears. Cover photo by
Hank Kranzler, courtesy of Stanford University Archives.

Contents

Preface   vii

Introduction   1

1   Classical Theatre   29

2   Medieval Theatre   51

3   Renaissance Theatre   65

4   Baroque Theatre   91

5   Eighteenth Century Theatre   115

6   Romantic Theatre   129

7   Realistic Theatre   145

8   Symbolist Theatre   167

9   Relativist Theatre   189

10   The New Theatre   215

Bibliography   221

Index   229

Preface

This book is an outgrowth of a text that I wrote in 1973, entitled *Stage Costume Design: Theory, Technique, and Style.* A number of students and colleagues who found my stylistic approach to costume design useful and interesting urged me to compress the major ideas and the pictures of that book into a small, cohesive volume that would be of practical service to all designers and directors interested in theatrical style in the western world. Thus encouraged, I distilled and rearranged my original ideas on costume design and applied them more broadly to theatre design and production.

During my years as a professional costume designer and student of the theatre, I came to realize, as a number of art critics and theatre historians have, that the compositional method or structural layout of a work of art is probably the most important element in determining the final style and character of the work. Because the compositional methods of playwrights and artists in each of the major periods of western cultural history were often similar despite the differences in media, I realized how much the theatre director and designer could gain by being able to perceive the similarities in compositional method between a play and a work of art composed during the same historical period. With this abstract knowledge, a designer does not need to illustrate a play by stage pictures based on factual knowledge of a period; instead, he can arrange color, space, mass, line, and texture on the stage in a way that reflects the compositional methods used by both the playwright and the other artists of the playwright's time. I have found this approach very useful even when my director has wished to work against this compositional method or structural style in his production, for it has enabled me to feel secure as a designer about the style and compositional method in the playscript before coping with a totally new and different artistic approach.

In each chapter of the book I discuss the art and culture of a major historical period, the developments in theatre and in dramatic method that took place, and at least one play representative of the period. The plays chosen are famous and frequently anthologized dramas that serve as clear examples of particular period styles or particular aspects of a period style, and reinforce the discussion of a visual approach to theatre design.

My intention in writing this book was to provide both students and teachers of scenic design and drama classes with a basic foundation for planning the style of a theatre production. I have presupposed that my readers have some knowledge of art and theatre history; this book will therefore meet the needs of intermediate to advanced courses in theatre design and drama, rather than introductory courses, where basic fundamentals form the course content.

I set forth in this book ideas that have evolved during my twenty-eight years of experience as a designer of costumes and a teacher of design and theatre history. Other ideas in the book have come from my students and colleagues who were either directly or indirectly involved with me in the theatre and in the classroom before and during the writing of this book. To these many individuals I am grateful. I am personally indebted to my teachers Virginia Opsvig, Hubert Heffner, and Frank Bevan, who instilled in me a desire to communicate my ideas on visual design; to my friend Lewis Spitz of the Stanford University History

Department, who encouraged my original desire to write; and to the staffs of the many libraries and museums in both the United States and Europe who allowed me to use the illustrations in the book. I would also like to express gratitude to Bea Gruen of the American Conservatory Theatre for her help with certain photos, and to the people at Mayfield Publishing Company—Lansing Hays, Marjorie Cutler, Michelle Hogan, Pamela Trainer, Carole Norton and Nancy Sears—for their thoughtful and painstaking assistance. I wish to thank particularly Norman Philbrick, former chairman of the Department of Drama at Stanford University, for both his kindness in allowing me to use illustrative material from his extensive theatre library and his advice and encouragement during the writing of the manuscript. Finally, I wish to thank my wife, Marilyn, for her helpful advice and editorial assistance.

Introduction

That theatre workers frequently disagree on the choice and execution of a particular style for a theatre production is not surprising. The style of a theatrical design is the ultimate expression of a complex of factors: the designer's individual temperament, his understanding of the compositional qualities of a play, and his knowledge of the relationship between the visual arts and the playwrights of a period. In my opinion, the designer should try to articulate an approach to theatre design that is an artistic interweaving of the form and structure of the play with a visual interpretation of space, shapes, lines, textures, and colors.

After three quarters of a century of abstraction in the visual arts, one point should be obvious: in theatre design, as in painting, sculpture, and the minor arts, the finished product in no way reproduces the reality of a particular period. Clearly, all that is ever presented on the stage, even when the designer insists that he is recording and presenting facts from life, is a personal interpretation of visual reality. The designer's style, influenced by the culture in which he lives, makes it impossible to set upon the stage exact visual phenomena from another era.

From the most primitive times, art has been limited, controlled, and

defined by the technical experience of the artist. Nature offers the artist only the raw materials for visual interpretation; the artist modifies the raw material by his craft, the medium in which he creates. Today, the theatre designer is strongly influenced by synthetics, new uses of materials and new discoveries in lighting and lighting control. His response to modern trends in the other visual arts will and should take precedence over the creation of authenticity and so-called period accuracy in the design of settings and costumes. Authenticity invariably lacks artistry, yet there are still people who confuse art and archaeology, and allow their admiration for scientific research to interfere with their intuitive reaction to an artistic experience.

The nineteenth century, for example, was an era when producers believed that fidelity to the facts of the past was both possible and desirable in theatrical production. In many a production that was intended to be a complete, annotated, visual tableau of some past time that would educate the public as much as it would entertain them, the final result was a piling up of authentic detail without capturing the cultural values of the period. Producers would often append pages of notes to their programs to place the full research that had gone into a production into the hands of the audience, and would claim that attending one of their productions was worth a week of study in the British Museum. But unfortunately, as any student of aesthetics knows, one cannot recreate the past, which is always seen through the eyes of the present. The designer and director who think they are being completely faithful to history by concentrating on historical detail are only undermining their play and its compositional values. A nineteenth century play based on the life of Queen Elizabeth, when presented on the stage, tells us more about nineteenth century theatrical taste than about life in the sixteenth century (Fig. 1).

Even after great designers like Adolphe Appia and Gordon Craig at the beginning of the twentieth century proved that mood and abstract

Figure 1
Mrs. D. P. Bowers as Queen Elizabeth in an 1888 production of a nineteenth century historical drama about the virgin queen. Note the ambiguities in costume created by combining elements of authentic Elizabethan dress with Victorian fashion lines. Photo from Paul Gebbie and Howard Gebbie, eds., *The Stage and Its Stars,* vol. 2. Courtesy Norman Philbrick Library

suggestion were far more important in theatre design than any realistic attempts to recreate the past, showmen from David Belasco to Cecil B. De Mille still attempted to press spectacular realism on their audiences. What resulted was a transparent falseness of feeling and effect, a second-hand product that was neither artistic nor unified, and lacked any overall sense of style. Art filters life. Any recreation of the past is doomed to failure because the artist cannot escape his own time and himself.

If we accept the idea that a production is designed to illuminate the compositional plan or scheme of a play, then arguments about whether one should always produce Shakespearean drama in Elizabethan dress disappear. The discussion shifts to how one can relate the use of line, texture, and color to the way the playwright has organized his plot, characters, dialogue, theme, rhythm, and spectacle. Thus when one designs *Hamlet*, it is the tone and structure of the drama, more than the period or the story, that should effect the design.

According to this approach, the designer does not work for story-telling and character values alone; he analyzes the plot to see how scenes are developed, how lines of action are intertwined, whether transitions are abrupt or smooth, whether scene contrasts are sharp or subtle. He examines the characterization of the play to see whether one character dominates, two antagonists rise above all others, or a group or a series of paired individuals is central to the play. He analyzes dialogue to see whether it is rich or spare, full of imagery or sharply telegraphic, tightened into quick character exchange, or expanded into long individual speeches. He will explore the theme and rhythmic progression of the play for qualities that could be translated into visual terms. For example, the theme of Genêt's *The Blacks* involves the contrast of black and white

Figure 2
A scene from Molière's *Tartuffe,* produced by the Stanford Repertory Theatre, Stanford University, 1965. An example of strong unity and simplicity in costume and setting based on the structure of the play. Photo by author

Figure 3
A scene from *Tartuffe,* produced by the American Conservatory Theatre, 1967, under the direction of William Ball. Costumes by Jane Greenwood. Sets by Stuart Wurzell. Photo by Hank Kranzler, San Francisco, California

races, and a designer can make excellent use of this color contrast in his designs. Thus in the end, the designer, with the aid of visual information given by the playwright and assisted by his analysis of the play's structure, prepares a design scheme that in its use of line, texture, and color combines abstract compositional information with the required visualization of the play's story.

When the director and designer discuss the design scheme for a production, they should stress the visual projection of the inner nature of the play, not period illustration. For example, it is the spare, simple, clean-cut plotting and direct characterization that are all important in the design of Molière's *Misanthrope* or *Tartuffe* (Figs. 2 and 3). Producing these plays with the fashionable clothing and rich architectural interiors of the French seventeenth century will indicate only that a designer has an extensive background in the age of Louis XIV. Once authenticity is put aside in the theatre design, the question of artistic style becomes complicated, yet artistically challenging.

How does the designer actually approach the problem of making visual equivalents that will throw light on the manner in which a playwright perceived and developed his material? Heinrich Wölfflin, in his *Principles of Art History,* set up five opposing modes of perception (polarities) to explain the differences between Renaissance and Baroque art. We can use these polarities to explain and organize the art of all periods, and, by extension, to understand the literary in relation to the visual arts. It is in this last sense that such formal comparisons may be useful to the student of theatre design, who must always be making a translation from a literary script to a visual production.

Wölfflin's first polarity is that between the linear and the painterly. A linear style emphasizes clarity of contour and the decorative isolation of ornamental details; a painterly style blurs the edges, merges objects, and gives an illusory and shifting appearance to objects. Thus, Botticelli's style is linear, Rembrandt's style is painterly (Figs. 4 and 5); Michelangelo's *David* is linear, Rodin's *Balzac* is painterly. Apply this concept to the theatre, and Racine's works are linear, Shakespeare's painterly.

Figure 4
Botticelli. *Judith with the Head of Holofernes,* ca. 1475.
An example of linear compositional method. Courtesy Alinari, Florence

Figure 5
Rembrandt. *The Denial of St. Peter,* ca. 1660. An
example of a painterly approach in brushwork and
compositional method. Courtesy Rijksmuseum,
Amsterdam

Wölfflin's second polarity is the distinction between depth in plane and depth in recession in the organization of compositional space. In depth in plane, space is organized as a series of receding planes; in recessional depth, the sense of plane is broken and visual space goes back in depth on diagonal and sharply foreshortened lines. For example, Ghiberti's panels for the second set of bronze doors for the Baptistry in Florence were organized to give depth in plane; depth in recession can be seen in the paintings of Rubens (Figs. 6 and 7). The same contrast can be seen in the way space is organized in early Renaissance architecture, with its depth in plane and in Baroque architecture, with its recessional depth. In the theatre, depth in plane and depth in recession can be seen by comparing *Romeo and Juliet* and *Hamlet*. The former projects a series of horizontal actions on a series of shallow planes against a rather flat background of city architecture or interiors. The latter involves Hamlet in action that moves from forward soliloquy directly back into full-scale court scenes, while the space and background around him create a labyrinthine illusion of great depth.

Figure 6
Ghiberti. *Solomon Receiving the Queen of Sheba,* from
"The Gates of Paradise," ca. 1430–1450. An example
of action in a series of shallow, receding, horizontal
planes. Courtesy Alinari, Florence

Figure 7
Rubens. *The Antwerp Adoration,* ca. 1620–1625. An
example of intensely swelling, recessional action
projecting out toward the viewer. Courtesy Royal
Museum, Antwerp

A third polarity involves closed versus open composition. In closed composition, objects are rigidly framed and enclosed, while in open composition, they are merged with outside space. Closed composition suggests a stable, limited, unchanging world; open composition, a world that flows on into infinity or into a realm beyond the known work. Leonardo's *The Last Supper* is certainly closed, while El Greco's *View of Toledo* is open (Figs. 8 and 9). In the theatre one can contrast the pictorial illusion framed by the proscenium with a production scheme that moves out into the audience. This polarity is reflected in the tight classical comedies of the Renaissance as opposed to the operatic productions of the Baroque, where the members of the corps de ballet moved down the steps at the front of the stage onto the floor of the auditorium.

Figure 8
Leonardo da Vinci. *The Last Supper,* 1494–1498. An example of closed composition. Courtesy Alinari, Florence

Figure 9
El Greco. *View of Toledo,* 1604–1614. An example of open composition. Courtesy The Metropolitan Museum of Art. Bequest of Mrs. H. O. Havemeyer, 1929. The H. O. Havemeyer Collection

Figure 10
Bramante. Tempietto. In the cloister of San Pietro in Montorio, Rome, 1502. An example of multiplicity of individual details. Courtesy Alinari, Florence

Figure 11
Borromini. The Church of San Carlino alle Quattro Fontane, Rome, 1638–1667. An example of compressed complex unity. Courtesy Alinari, Florence

Another polarity, which is as vividly apparent in theatre as in art, is that between multiplicity of incident or effect and compressed unity. In the former, individual details retain their identity while fitting harmoniously into a whole, while in the latter the details disappear and the individual elements cannot be distinguished. This contrast is particularly clear when one compares High Renaissance and Baroque architecture. In Bramante's Tempietto in Rome the separate parts are organized harmoniously, while in Borromini's Church of San Carlino alle Quattro Fontane, it is difficult to see where one effect stops and another begins (Figs. 10 and 11). Most "classical" plays demand visual effects in which each part is seen for its own effect; in "romantic" plays the details are lost in the rich overall picture.

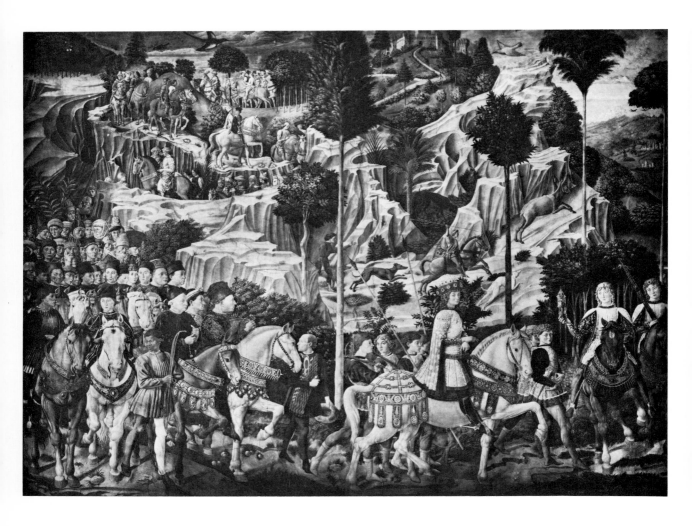

Wölfflin's last polarity is between relative and absolute clarity, a contrast similar to that between painterly and linear, but stressing light rather than composition. The light and color of a painting, statue, or building may be used to clarify and illuminate or to blur and distort, until strong images are reduced to flickering, subjective symbols that stir the imagination and the beholder's sense of the mysterious. Visual examples might be an outdoor scene such as that in Gozzoli's *Journey of the Magi,* which is an example of absolute clarity, and El Greco's *View of Toledo* which is an example of relative clarity (Figs. 12 and 9). In the theatre the lighting designer can manipulate this polarity, as can costume and set designers, by using surfaces and textures to absorb and reflect light.

Other polarities can of course, be developed. For example, Wylie Sypher, in *Four Stages of Renaissance Style,* makes a case for a distinction between art that is in phase with culture and reality and art that is out of phase—broken in its rhythms and distorted in its overall effect; El Greco's *View of Toledo* is an example of the latter while Raphael's *School of Athens* exemplifies the former. There is the basic contrast between art that is fully at rest, for example, the paintings of Poussin, and art that is constantly in motion, such as the paintings of Rubens. In the theatre the slow, almost static pace of Racine can be compared with the full movement of Shakespeare. Or there is the very simple contrast, which has been at the heart of much controversy during the past 100 years, between a representational and a nonrepresentational depiction of nature. Or again there is the strong contrast between art that appeals to the eye and art that appeals to the touch—visual versus tactile art. One can also contrast the geometric organization of a work of art with free organization—Mondrian versus Miró, or the balanced, geometric symmetry of *Romeo and Juliet* versus the free organization of *Measure for Measure* (Figs. 13 and 14). There is also the contrast between the dark and light in art—between Botticelli and Rembrandt (see Figs. 4 and 5), or between *Macbeth* and *Two Gentlemen of Verona.* In composition or stage blocking there is the con-

Figure 12
Gozzoli. *The Journey of the Magi,* 1459. An example of absolute clarity in painting. Courtesy Alinari, Florence

Figure 13
Mondrian. *Composition, 1936.* An example of geometric composition. Courtesy Philadelphia Museum of Art: The Louise and Walter Arensberg Collection

Figure 14
Miró. *Carnival of Harlequin,* ca. 1925. An example of free-field organization. Courtesy Albright-Knox Gallery, Buffalo, New York, Room of Contemporary Art Fund

trast between the balance and equilibrium of horizontal and vertical energies, as in a painting by Botticelli, and the oblique angles and spiraling effects in the mannerist art of Tintoretto.

An understanding of all these contrasts, although they may not fully explain changes of style, certainly assists the designer and director in discussing and pinpointing the particular style of the production on which they are to collaborate.

A student of design will also have a better feeling for how his art is tied to the history of the visual arts if he understands to some extent the pattern of the artistic pendulum that swings from abstraction to reality, from the irrational to the rational, and back again. There has always been a tendency for man to turn from a stress on the intuitive, the emotional,

and the irrational, to the analytical, the intellectual, and the rational in the visual arts; from the wish for submission to the mystery and reality of an impenetrable world to the desire to organize and control that world. For example, the great contrast between Paleolithic and Neolithic art stems from this shift in emphasis. The Paleolithic cave paintings of southern France and northern Spain present a striking naturalism—an attempt to identify directly with the animal portrayed in order to capture and kill it. These paintings were a form of sympathetic magic by which primitive man became a part of the mystery of the natural world (Fig. 15). But when man began to control nature and organize life, he exerted his will over the forces of nature. Neolithic art reduced nature to simple diagrams that stressed rationality, structure, organization, and the regularization of the seemingly accidental effects in nature and life. Art thus became a celebration of man's power over nature (Fig. 16). In the western world, from Greek times to the present, we can observe cycles of development that swing from the rational to the irrational and back again.

Ever since a cohesive cultural style disappeared with the Rococo and artists became self-conscious about their own personal style and its relation to other artistic styles past and present, there has been a proliferation of "isms" in both theatre and art. Most of these isms can be ranged in groups around the two polarities in man's response to the universe: the rational and the irrational, or, to speak in terms current for the past 200 years, the classical and the romantic. *Classical* describes a work that stresses order, structure, logic, simplicity, and the rationality of form; *romantic* describes a work that is rich in emotion, sensuous appeal, and complex action. Once these stylistic polarities are set in the consciousness, then expressionism, impressionism, surrealism, symbolism, naturalism, and realism can be grouped in relation to them.

Figure 15
Polychrome bison from the caves of Altamira in northern Spain, ca. 50,000–8,000 B.C. An example of naturalism in Paleolithic art. Courtesy Spanish National Tourist Office

Figure 16
Figures on the skin of a Lapp drum from northern Sweden, ca. 1800 A.D. An example of the abstract geometric qualities in Neolithic art. Courtesy Museum für Völkerkunde, Munich

Expressionism will almost always be accepted as an abstraction from reality, will tend more toward the emotional than the rational, and can be thought of as an exaggerated statement of inner psychological reality instead of an outward realism. Impressionism will at times be accepted as reality, but impressionistic style usually moves to a level of abstraction, with a strong element of subtle, intuitive emotionalism and a weak or vague compositional form. Surrealism, which is not well represented in the drama, makes use of the dreams and sensations of the inner mind and has sensational or romantic overtones. By its nature it will not be accepted as a representation of reality. Naturalism hugs close to the actual life from which it is derived and has few strongly identifiable characteristics, while realism tends to be more selectively developed, organizing and balancing the rational and irrational poles in life. Both of these stylistic forms are representational in intent and do not allow the audience to be strongly aware of the compositional methods of the artist. Symbolism may stress either the rational or the irrational, the representational or the nonrepresentational, but can always be recognized by the heavy and somewhat obvious use of symbols in the material presented. Mannerism is derived from a sixteenth century artistic term and is used in the twentieth century to describe any art that suggests an ambiguous, distorted, and unbalanced inner world behind the real one. Even when tightly and rationally organized, mannerist style is meant to be accepted intuitively.

Although all theatre productions are by nature unreal or abstracted from reality to some extent, there is a whole class of theatre productions whose intention is to represent life in such a way as to have the audience accept what is seen as a picture of reality. The point at which theatre designers begin to abstract and organize this reality for obvious artistic effect is always difficult to define, but, if one draws a line that moves toward pure abstraction from exact reality, there is a point beyond which the audience will see and accept what is seen as an artistic abstraction.

The theatre designer must always make a choice between using visual material to illuminate directly, or to comment on and illuminate subtly, a particular period in terms of story and character. The twentieth century has certainly made it very popular to design abstractly, but the visual abstractions should still be at the service of the drama. A production can be as close to reality or as far from it as the director, the designer, and the playwright wish, as long as the impossible is not attempted: the re-creation of the past or the present. Many a brilliant and unified production may give the audience the illusion of a past period, but careful analysis will prove that space, shapes, lines, textures, and colors have been interpreted from the point of view of the designer to create the world of the play before creating the period in which the play was written. Even a well-designed "realistic" production will create the world of the play before creating time and place in a past era. The audience may be completely unaware of the designer's manipulation of artistic values, however, and accept the whole as a statement of reality. On the other hand, a designer frequently designs what he would call a "stylized" production, in which he stresses line, texture, and color at the expense of visual reality—only to find the audience accepting the entire scheme as a representation of period reality. The response of an audience depends greatly on their knowledge of visual processes, their educational and intellectual level, and on the visual values stressed in their culture.

When one sets a play, for the sake of mere novelty, in a period other than that in which the play was written, the superficial result will usually detract from the drama. If the structure and tone of the play are kept in mind in the choices of line, texture, and color made from the new period, however, then the new period can usually be successfully fitted to the play. What if the director is using the play as a mere libretto for his own artistic interpretation—the presentation of a production that may have little relationship to the script written by the playwright? The designer must follow his director and let the audience and critics decide whether the new production is better than the old, a distortion of the playwright's intent, or a fascinating but not necessarily helpful look at an old drama. Even in the wildest of directorial deviations from a script, however, the designer should understand the nature of the play from which he and his director are working. Only when a designer has a secure feeling for the relationship between the visual arts of a period and the playwrights of that era is he really ready to work with a director for special emphases, shifts in period, or distortions and exaggerations to bring new light to a drama (Fig. 17).

The theatrical designer is an interpreter of another man's artistic product, not a fine artist who begins with his own artistic ideas, and to force a personal style on each production that one designs is basically dishonest. What is needed is a fusion of all that can be learned about a play and its background with the visual sources and design concepts that are prevalent today. The designer must search for the modern style equivalent for what he finds in his research into the past. Since the designer usually works with the limitations set by his script, only when he is designing for some entertainment or ceremonial occasion is he free to create like the painter, the sculptor, or the architect. There are occasions, however, when even these artists are required to work under strong limitations, and we might take example from their solutions to problems on such occasions to indicate how the theatrical designer may solve his artistic problems within the style limitations of a script.

Let us use as an example the architect who must fit his design into a group of buildings constructed in an earlier era. No self-respecting architect today would design a structure that recreated all the attributes of some historical style. He would study the style of the older buildings, use the abstract attributes of line, texture, and color to design a structure that would harmonize with the older buildings, and interpret space, form, and surface texture in terms of contemporary visual usage. At Stanford University in Stanford, California, several new buildings have been erected in which the red tile roofs, sandstone texture, round arches, and cloistered porticoes have been retained from the original Richardson-Romanesque style of the 1880s. In each new structure the basic characteristics of the older buildings have been retained while new visual modes have been strongly stressed. Arches are simpler, smoother, and unornamented; surfaces are smooth plaster or poured concrete rather

Figure 17
The husband and wife in *There and Back* (*Hin und Zurück*), a comic opera by Hindemith produced by the Stanford Opera Theatre, Stanford University, 1962. An example of distortion and exaggeration to match the score and libretto. Photo by author

Introduction

22

Introduction

24

than cut stone; there is a sense of thrust and balance in the distribution of mass rather than piled-up block forms; and an overall cleanness of form replaces the variety of carved stone effects in the original. Yet with all the simplifications, expansions, and contractions of form in relation to space, the basic idea of a tile-roofed, sandstone structure surrounded by round arches has been retained (Fig. 18).

Theatrical design today should take advantage of the same dual effect: beautiful in its own right as a modern design yet with reference to the forms and usages of the past from which the particular play derives. In a Shakespearean production, for example, one may spatter and spray the costumes, use twisted and melted steel in the set, and treat synthetic fabrics with heat and chemicals to gain new textural forms and create modern equivalents of the visual and textural uses of mannerism, the style prevalent in Europe when Shakespeare wrote his plays. There are no rules, no ways in which to know how little or how much to change and develop sources; that depends upon sensitivity, intuition, and feeling for the original sources as well as for modern artistic ideals, and on a complete and thorough sense of communication with the director.

An actual style approach to a production of Aeschylus' *Prometheus Bound,* presented by the Stanford Repertory Theatre in 1966, may be useful as an example at this point. The director wanted to use a visual presentation that would stress primitive ritual and ceremony, and he decided that the characters, none of whom was specifically human, should suggest natural organic substances grouped about a towering central rock. An illustration of a piece of malachite in a book on precious stones finally helped the scene designer to develop a Y-shaped rock in the crotch of which Prometheus would be bound and symbolically re-born. The shape of the central rock was reflected in the conical silhouettes of the chorus costumes, which were constructed of overlapping petals developed from a cross-section of the blue and green malachite

Figure 18
The Lou Henry Hoover Pavilion of The Hoover Institution, Stanford University. An example of the tile roofs, and columns and arches of the Richardson Romanesque architecture of the old campus at Stanford used in a contemporary architectural design. Photo by author

shot with white, suggesting the sea as it laps against a rocky shore—an appropriate image for a chorus that represents the daughters of Oceanus. The chorus costumes were made of melted nylon to give the corruscated texture of rock and seaweed, while the rock in the center of the stage was covered with crinkled metal foil under cheesecloth painted in blues, greens and browns. The masks reflected primitive images from the South Pacific as well as Greek theatrical usage. Thus the stage plan, masks, and body forms reflected both the primitive origins of the Greek drama and the textures, colors, and shapes that would appeal to contemporary visual sensibilities (Fig. 19).

Figure 19
A scene from *Prometheus Bound* by Aeschylus, produced by the Stanford Repertory Theatre, Stanford University, 1966. An example of traditional Greek masks and costumes interpreted in terms of primitive, ritualistic evocations of natural organic forms.
Photo by Hank Kranzler, San Francisco, California

1

Classical Theatre

Theatre developed out of primitive rituals performed by man to influence nature and probe the seemingly unanswerable questions about his universe. As these rituals became more and more complex, many theatrical effects, such as body movement, vocal chanting, storytelling, and special dress, make-up, and accessories, were used in the ceremonies. With his ability to perform before others, disguised as an animal or a god, man had sown the seeds of theatrical presentation. The myths and legends that eventually developed from these rituals bore a close rhythmic, sequential, and verbal relationship to the way the primitive tribe actually lived. In the performance of rituals rhythmic dance movement projected "man in action" before the gods; the mask was the key visual accessory for doing business with the world of the spirit.

The kinds of complex headdresses and masked faces used in both early and contemporary ritual range from birds emerging from the head, suggesting the flight of the inner soul, to masks with a fantastic variety of decorations around the eyes, the windows to the soul. In all masked figures the stress is on the face and torso rather than on the limbs of the human figure, and the total visual effect is usually awesome and frightening—a projection of the unrestrained imagination of primitive man (Fig. 20).

Figure 20
A mask of the Basonge Tribe of the Belgian Congo.
Courtesy Stanford University Art Department

Figure 21
Oceanus from *Prometheus Bound* by Aeschylus, produced by the Stanford Repertory Theatre, Stanford
University, 1966. An example of marine forms and
textures used to create a ritualistic ceremonial
costume. Photo by Hank Kranzler, San Francisco,
California

Figure 22
Model of the Parthenon in Athens, 447–432 B.C.
The finest example of Greek classical architecture,
which balances highly subtle and sophisticated
proportions with very simple and natural forms.
Courtesy The Metropolitan Museum of Art. Purchase, 1890, Levi Hale Willard Bequest

It is from these primitive rituals with masks that most aspects of the written drama developed; in the elementary, rustic form of Greek tragedy, the mask was all-important in projecting the religious and mysterious aspects of the drama. In a production of a Greek play, such as *Prometheus Bound* by Aeschylus, a director may stress, as the Dutch director Erik Vos did for a production at the Stanford Repertory Theatre in 1966, the primitive visual aspects of ritual rather than the more sophisticated playwriting technique in the script. By visualizing each human form as a symbolic evocation of some elemental, organic earth spirit, Vos, in this case, gained in visual power what may have been lost in intellectual subtlety (Fig. 21).

Although the Greek Dionysiac festivals devoted to dramatic performances were held in honor of Dionysus, the god of irrationality, Greek drama itself concentrated on a balance of human and natural forces. Indeed, the balance between natural freedom and man-made control, between democratic individualism and aristocratic organization exemplified the "golden age" of fifth century B.C. Greek culture (Fig. 22). When individualism and particularism began to triumph in art and life at the close of the fifth century, classical balance and idealization began to falter and disappear.

In fifth century Greek tragedy, problems of current politics were usually projected against a mythical background, and the religious bases of the stories made the plays an excellent ground for the mediation of conflict between religion and state policy, religion and art, and the rational and the irrational in the Greek spirit. The rational spirit, represented by Apollo, god of light, was as fundamental to tragedy as the spirit of religious fervor and irrationality, represented by the god Dionysus. As tragedy developed, the rational element became paramount in the structure and plot, while the irrational lay below the surface of the play and in the questioning tone of the chorus.

The chorus in Greek tragedy was the backbone of the tragedy and a key factor in determining the original arrangement and development of the performance area. Working as a group in a circular orchestra in front of the *skene,* a structure that served as both a dressing room and a background for a play's action, the chorus and actors performed the plays before thousands of spectators seated in the three-quarter circle of seats that spread up the slopes of the hillside (Fig. 23). Scenic effects were limited to changes that transformed the façade of the *skene* from a palace into a temple or some other dwelling, and to mechanical devices that could bring gods, ghosts, and dead bodies onto the stage, or reveal to the audience what was happening behind the scene. The chorus and three actors projected the most impressive visual effects through the precision and complexity of their movements. Dressed in long-sleeved, full-length tunics or chitons with full-draped folds and decorated with symbolic ornaments, and crowned with cork masks that reflected the grandeur as well as the subtlety found in the sculpted head of Poseidon of Cape Artemision (Fig. 24), the Greek actor in action must have been an imposing sight. The costume allowed for great flexibility and freedom of movement; only at a much later date did enlarged masks with violently exaggerated expressions, raised shoes, and padded shoulders create the puppetlike effect that is so frequently seen in certain twentieth century

Classical Theatre

Figure 23
Drawing of a reconstruction of a fifth century Greek theater. Courtesy Stanford University Art Department

Classical Theatre

33

Figure 24
Poseidon of Artemision, ca. 460–450 B.C. One of the finest examples of fifth century transitional or severe classical style. Courtesy Hirmer Fotoarchiv, Munich

Figure 25
Creon returns triumphantly from the shrine of Apollo in the Tyrone Guthrie Theater's 1972 production of *Oedipus Rex*, directed by Michael Langham, translated and adapted by Anthony Burgess, designed by Desmond Heeley, with music by Stanley Silverman. Courtesy The Guthrie Theater, Minneapolis, Minnesota

productions of Greek tragedy. Recent productions of *Oedipus Rex* have tended to stress primitive simplicity and ritual mystery (Fig. 25).

Why should the Poseidon of Cape Artemision speak to us more directly as a visual image of a mask used in productions of Aeschylean tragedy than all the information we can derive from historical facts about Greek masks? The answer is that this head of Poseidon represents visually the culmination of the so-called severe style in fifth century sculpture, a style that developed at the same time that Aeschylus was

completing his last great plays. The structure, planning, outlook, characterization, even the rhythms in the plays of Aeschylus and in the visual arts of the mid-fifth century were similar. Studying the compositional methods of both tragedy and the visual arts will enable the student of design to make the right visual choices for his design of sets and costumes for an Aeschylean tragedy. We can also view Sophocles' outlook and method in relation to the shift from the severe to the mature classical style in the visual arts of the mid-fifth century (Fig. 26), and Euripides', outlook and method in relation to the personal and individual styles that developed after the close of the fifth century, culminating in the theatrical effects of Hellenistic art (Fig. 27). Each playwright's compositional method reflected the changes developing in the visual arts at the same time; a designer for a contemporary production of a Greek tragedy can profit far more from studying the plays in relation to the visual arts than by limiting his knowledge to the fifth century Greek theatre.

While tragedy was developing at the hands of Aeschylus, Sophocles, and Euripides, Old Comedy matured at the hand of Aristophanes, the only Greek comic poet whose complete plays we have. Many of Aristophanes' plays dealt with the political and social problems of his day. Although his comedies defy full translation, Aristophanes' genius for bawdy, topical, and sophisticated satire was so strong that his best plays, with their original spirit of exuberance and wild humor, still captivate audiences. Many of the plays took their names from the disguises assumed by the chorus—*Knights, Wasps, Birds, Clouds,* and *Frogs*—and it was primarily through the songs of the chorus that Aristophanes projected his satire. The basic idea in each play was comic in itself (for example, the staging of a sex strike to bring an end to the war in the *Lysistrata*) and was reinforced by a series of separate humorous scenes that gave great scope to both the comic inventiveness of the playwright and the acting abilities of the individual performers. A modern playwright could not hope to be accepted by a popular audience if he combined the personal invective, social satire, slapstick comedy, and obscenity that we

Figure 26
The Dying Niobid, ca. 450–440 B.C. An example of
fifth century high classical Greek sculpture. Courtesy
Alinari, Florence

Classical Theatre

37

find in the majority of the plays of Aristophanes. Although a modern audience cannot appreciate all of the political and social illusions in these plays, it can enjoy the outrageous and universal sense of fun and the bawdy physical comedy in each play when it is projected by superior actors.

The basic structure of the plays of Aristophanes was simple. A prologue established the mood and presented the comic idea, such as stopping a war by having all of the women in the *Lysistrata* go on strike. The chorus then entered, often wearing masks and grotesque dresses to suit their roles, and a debate took place about the merits of the comic idea. In a choral ode the chorus directly addressed the audience about some current political or social problem and urged the members of the audience to take a particular stand. The second part of the play consisted of a series of loosely connected episodes that demonstrated the results of accepting the comic idea. The last scene reconciled all characters before they exited to a banquet or feast.

Toward the middle of the fourth century B.C., New Comedy began to replace Old Comedy. Themes of romance and of personal and domestic problems replaced the themes of social and political problems, and characters became more common types drawn from contemporary society.

Let us now go back to Sophocles and analyze his *Oedipus Rex* in terms of its compositional method and then relate this analysis to the problems of visual production. Although the myth on which the play is based is quite complex, the plot is very simple, events appear to be inevitable, the time on stage is actual time, and all the action takes place in one location. The playwright kept the primitive ancient rhythms inherent in the original myth and merged them with the rational organization of his dramatic form, deepening the tragic rhythm common to both. The situation as the play opens is analogous to the withering into winter in the ancient rituals of the seasons, followed by death and the hope for renewal. The play can also be understood as an exciting murder mystery with Oedipus

Figure 27
The Dying Gaul, Roman copy of a bronze original, ca. 230–220 B.C. This work represents the individualized and theatrical view in art and theatre during the Hellenistic period. Courtesy Alinari, Florence

as a prosecutor who finally convicts himself. As in the visual arts of fifth century Greece the concentration in *Oedipus Rex* on a simple and rationally perfect form leads to a heightened sense of nature and the mystery that lies behind it.

Sophocles was not interested in the details of the physical appearance, social position, or background of his characters, but in the psychological and ethical attributes that each carried in relation to the story. We know almost nothing about the characters. They are there simply to project several strong themes or ideas: no man can escape the pain of life until he has come to its end; man's vision is limited in the face of fate or the "will of the gods"; and to avoid fate is to invite divine retribution.

The language of the play is as spare, polished, and direct as the structure. The imagery is based on the main themes of the drama and carries the action from reason to passion, from ritual symbol to natural fact, from tragic poetry to direct prose. This variety of imagery supplies the actor with the histrionic possibilities that make the play so powerful in performance. The rhythm in the play is strong and insistent. It swings from forward movement to backward-looking exposition, which explores actions that took place prior to the play's action; the music and movement of the choral interludes punctuate and deepen the mood and mysterious atmosphere that lie behind and beneath the surface of the tragedy.

The visual demands of the play are sharply limited. The background is the palace, the costumes need project only the station of the character and his nobility of character, and the masks (if they are used) indicate only age and personality, with a change of mask for Oedipus when blinded. Most of the visual richness of a production would come from the patterns of movement in the chorus in relation to the actors.

The first decision that a director faces with his designer in a production of *Oedipus Rex* is whether to emphasize the rational or the irrational elements in the play. Given the choice today between the classical restraint and formality of the play's structure and the ritualistic, violent,

Classical Theatre

Figure 28
Ken Ruta as the blind Teresias in the American Conservatory Theatre's 1970 production of *Oedipus Rex,* directed by William Ball, designed by Robert Fletcher. Courtesy William Ganslen, photographer, San Francisco, California

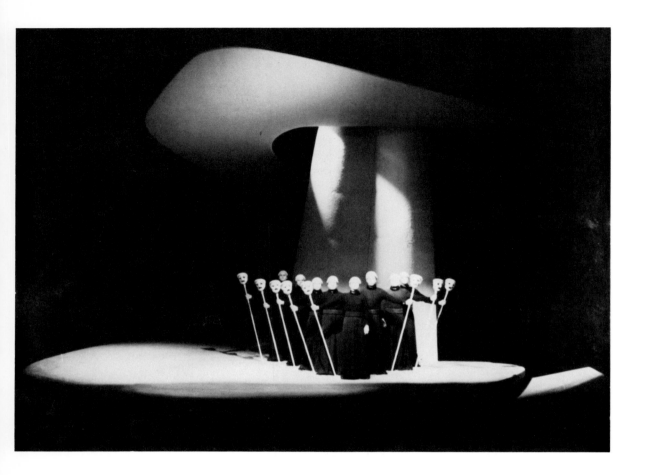

Classical Theatre

42

primitive aspects of the script, most modern directors would choose the latter. Rather than ask for a completely formal palace constructed of smooth textures and balanced forms, the contemporary English and American director and designer will more often choose rough textures, broken forms, muted colors, and exaggerated and even grotesque effects in masks or make-up to stress the primitive, ritual background of the drama (Fig. 28). Occasionally on the Continent, where cool intellectual, classical productions are more common and more admired, a designer will design the play using modern visual effects equivalent to the mature classical style of mid-fifth century Greek art (Fig. 29).

A designer could achieve a balance between the rational and the irrational elements found in the script by arranging symmetrically the space for the play's action, with the palace placed squarely behind the chorus, and by manipulating movement, masks, fabric textures, wall surfaces, and shapes to project the mysterious, primitive, and ceremonial elements in the drama. If masks cannot be used because of the closeness of the actors to an audience in a small theatre or performance space, the make-up should be heightened to project the symbolic as well as the realistic aspects of a role; if masks are used they should relate (even when abstracted and unreal) to that balance of form and expression found in the heads of Greek statuary of the mid-fifth century. To use masks that are too archaic and formal, as many were in the famed Stratford, Ontario, production of 1955, is to lose subtlety and depth of character (Fig. 30).

Since the robes worn by Greek actors and members of the chorus in classical times completely covered their bodies, both to enable three actors to play all the roles and to make the idealized, symbolic aspect of a character as strong as the individualized and personal aspect, there is merit in retaining this visual effect in a contemporary production. By concentrating the attention of the audience on both the mask and the movement of the body under the soft, supple, draped lines of the robes, audience response will be less to the tactile, the human, and the natural,

Figure 29
A stage model designed by Franz Mertz for a production of *Oedipus Rex*, produced at the Landestheater, Darmstadt, Germany, 1952. Courtesy Staatstheater Darmstadt

and more to the ethical, the ideal, and the ritualistic. In Greek art, color, although bright, was usually simple and direct, and subordinate to line, shape, and texture. Thus, in the costume designs for a production of *Oedipus Rex,* a limited range of colors should be used and each costume should be of a single color, with some use of neutral or metallic accents. Used in this way, color will give unity and atmosphere, rather than pictorial illustrations of character and story, and will allow for the strong three-dimensional lighting of the masks and the movement.

In the use of ornament a balance should be struck between the flat patterns that might be used on costume borders and the raised, three-dimensional patterns of pins, brooches, belts, and tiaras. Raised ornament can be used to give strength and focus to various parts of the costume.

The visual design for *Oedipus Rex* should be both ritualistic and mysterious, formal and natural. The challenge is to create a production that balances, with an appropriate tension, the ritualistic and formal aspects of the legend with the natural and deeply human psychological reality of the character relationships. Simple, symmetrical, richly textured settings, severe masks, and supple, draped costumes are the most direct means for achieving this balance.

Roman art and culture borrowed greatly from Greek art and culture, yet it had a character all its own. If we compare Greek sculpture, which was primarily for public display, with Roman sculpture, much of which was portraiture for private homes, we find that most Roman sculpture was far more naturalistic and less idealized than the Greek (Fig. 31). When Roman painting became more important than sculpture it too stressed naturalism and momentary illusionism.

The Roman comic writers Plautus and Terence imitated Greek New Comedy. Before the large permanent Roman theatres of the Empire were built, the performance of comedies took place on a long, narrow, temporary wooden platform bounded by a stage house at the back and sides; three doors in the back wall served as entrances to characters'

Figure 30
Douglas Campbell as Oedipus in the Tyrone Guthrie
Theater's 1955 production of *Oedipus Rex.* Courtesy
Stratford Shakespeare Festival, Stratford, Ontario,
Canada

houses. Most of the characters in the comedies of Plautus and Terence were stock personalities—old men, young lovers, and parasitical servants. Costumes were exaggerations from life, reflecting in color and line the "occupation" of the character. Wigs were conventionalized in color and grotesquely comic masks allowed a full range of parts for a single actor. The chorus appeared in very few plays. Some lyrical passages were sung by the actor, usually to the accompaniment of a flute. The problems presented were neither ethical nor political, but domestic, involving mistaken identities, lost children, forced marriages, and parental obtuseness. The most important character was almost invariably the comic slave. Names such as *Peniculus* (the broom), *Erotium* (sensuality), *Cylindrus* (the rolling pin), were descriptive of either personality or profession.

In Plautus' *Menaechmi,* a comedy about the mistaken identities of twin brothers, the dialogue is direct and utilitarian, used to further the plot, make comic descriptions, and project bawdy jokes. Comic effects are achieved by matching an expression, a word, or a brief visual description to a physical action. There is little sense of theme or idea in this play, merely a good humored cynicism about the ridiculous weaknesses of human character. The rhythm of the piece is fast paced, geared to the strenuous physical action of the play. The scenery requirements are minimal: a platform with the suggestion of houses at the rear and alcoves and projections for concealment and eavesdropping. Costumes should be exaggerated caricatures of the clothing worn in everyday society, whether that society is Roman or modern.

The first thing that strikes one about the *Menaechmi* is its similarity to a certain kind of modern musical. The songs, plot, rude jokes, and superficial sentiment remind one of musicals of the 1920s and 1930s that were dominated by vaudeville and burlesque. Whatever period a designer may choose for the play, he will want to design both sets and costumes with flat, bright colors, sharp outlines, exaggerated forms, and crisp, flat textures that one associates with cartoons, comic strips, and early twentieth century musical comedy. The play has been produced

Figure 31
Portrait of a Roman, ca. 80 B.C. An excellent example of solid realism in Roman sculpture. Courtesy Alinari, Florence

Figure 32
Costume sketches for the *Menaechmi* by Plautus.
By the author

Figure 33
Polychrome calyx krater showing a dancing phylax,
ca. 350–340 B.C. The *phylakes* comedies of southern
Italy were ribald travesties of mythological subjects
that heavily influenced Roman comedy. Courtesy
The Metropolitan Museum of Art, Rogers Fund,
1951.

with costumes, make-up, and settings based on the Charlie Brown comic strip, and the resultant designs were very successful (Fig. 32). The fluted columns of Roman architecture and draped Roman tunics would be out of place in a comic production unless they were sharply simplified or exaggerated. The short-phrased, rapid-fire dialogue should be reflected visually in sets and costumes: all costume and set lines should be short and broken; colors should be as hard and as loud as the boisterous action; ornamentation should be simple, large, and flat; and black outlines should be used to accentuate and create a strong sense of cartoon and flat illustration. The masks and wigs originally used in productions of Roman comedy would be effective in exaggerating character, but would also hide the comic expressions of the actors. The use of padding, which is very evident in Greek and Roman comic figurines, would not only contribute to caricature grotesqueness in a contemporary production, but also make the twins look more exactly alike. Sculpted figurines of characters in Greek New Comedy and vase paintings depicting rural farces and urban comedy can serve as inspirations for these effects (Fig. 33).

In a production of the *Menaechmi,* as in the productions of most Roman comedy, the visual equivalents to the compositional structure and characterization of the play are so insistent that the range of visual choices is effectively limited. A designer can create a contemporary visual effect while still retaining the abstract visual effects apparent in the script and used in original productions of Roman comedies.

Medieval Theatre

For many years medieval art and theatre have been viewed as a cultural backsliding from the naturalism, logic, and organization of Greek and Roman art and theatre, interrupted now and then by attempts to re-establish the art of antiquity—attempts which finally culminated in the Italian Renaissance. A closer view of the medieval mind and method, as we find in Henry Adams's *Mont St. Michel and Chartres,* shows us, however, that medieval art was so opposed to the logic and rationalism of antiquity that, even when it showed an interest in classical sources, the thought and ideals behind the art were logical only within the realm of a dual world comprising both heaven and earth—the world as interpreted by Thomas Aquinas and Dante. Medieval thought attempted to create a balance between the world of nature and the world of the spirit; the scholastic subtleties devised to bring order to this double world could not reduce the strain of contradiction between the spirit and the flesh. Dante saw the two poles clearly: the ideal order of a universe, expressing God's unchanging will, and the shifting life of human beings, caught in the pain of earthly existence. It is this double vision which was expressed in the great Gothic cathedrals—the aspiring, idealistic upward thrust of the buttresses and skeletal stonework attempting to overcome the solidity of walls and enclosed space, and the sense of strain and instability created by the combination of soaring towers and overreaching vaults (Fig. 34).

The true medieval spirit emerged in the Gothic period, when Gothic art gave man a more central place in nature than did Romanesque or Carolingian art. This growing humanism was always seen in relation to the hereafter and the divine, however, and there was always a conflict between the personal and the abstract, between the logical and the transcendental. Gothic architecture was so much a part of this conflict that it negated the very idea of architecture as the enclosing of space. By framing and penetrating space rather than defining or encompassing it, Gothic architecture merely enclosed sculpture and stained glass. Gothic cathedrals became illustrated books of knowledge for the religious community. The common man could "read" a Gothic cathedral inside and out in the glass and wood, and metal and stone, and find it crowded with intensely human anecdotes, stories, and details presented in a simple linear progression (Fig. 35). This simple linear progression was also present in Gothic literature, where compartmentalized scenes were presented one after another until a cycle of stories was completed. The stories lacked dramatic focus and a point of climax to which all characters and episodes converged because a one-dimensional storytelling or processional approach did not create a unified plot or scheme. Gothic art and literature gave us dramatic episodes with very human actors, but neither the stage nor the space for truly humanistic drama.

The revival of drama during the Middle Ages came with the development of dramatic interludes introduced into the church service at the beginning of the Romanesque period in the tenth century A. D. No one is exactly certain why this came about, but it seems probable that the Church hoped to make the lessons more vivid and interesting. Since most parishioners could not understand Latin, the short dramatic interpolations gave a direct visual statement of biblical stories.

The two most important dates in the church calendar were Christmas and Easter, and the strongest and most popular dramatizations grew up

Figure 34
Notre Dame Cathedral, Paris, 1163–1250. An example of transitional to High Gothic architecture. Courtesy French Government Tourist Office

Medieval Theatre

around these annual festivals. Later, when the Church moved the dramatized liturgical episodes to the square in front of the cathedral and set aside a specific festival week—the Festival of Corpus Christi—for the performance of mystery plays, the arrangement of the scenes inside the cathedral was retained in the general plan of the outdoor performances. What had been the altar area became the central point of focus, with little booths or "mansions" set up along the sides to echo the scene placement in the aisles of the cathedral. These mansions were identical in many ways to the little compartments or framing niches that surround the religious scenes and characters that adorn the inside and outside of the Gothic cathedral, and they vividly indicated the strong connections between art and drama in medieval culture. The area around the individual mansions was the neutral playing space, or *platea,* within which actors could move from one mansion to another as the action demanded (Fig. 36).

There were other variations besides the open layout in the cathedral square: a rectangular platform on which various mansions were arranged in linear progression from left to right; a pageant wagon that carried a two-storied mansion from square to square throughout the city until all the wagons had played to all audiences gathered for the occasion; and the use of ancient amphitheatres as a setting for a circular arrangement of mansions around a central platea. But always there were certain constraints: a series of mansions surrounded by generalized space; a series of short playlets tied together only by their placement in the Bible or in church literature; the frequent use of three planes of action—earth, heaven, and hell; and the attempt to make frightening and miraculous effects as convincing and realistic as possible (Fig. 37).

The major area of concentration in special effects was the hellmouth, with its fire and smoke, and the horrific reality of devils who emerged from it equipped with terrifying masks, tails, claws, hoofs, pitchforks, and exploding fireworks. Examples of costumes and accessories can be found in both the sculptural programs dealing with the Last Judgment and the gargoyles of Gothic cathedrals. The costumes for medieval plays

Figure 35
Annunciation to the Shepherd. From the Sacramentary of Fulda, Bamberg Library, Germany, second half of the eleventh century. An example of how properties and framing devices were used to present subject matter in "scenes." Courtesy Stanford University Art Department

Figure 36
Manuscript illumination of the stage of a passion
play produced at Valenciennes, France, 1547. The
various mansions, reading from left to right, represent paradise, Nazareth, the temple, Jerusalem, a
palace, the golden door, the sea, and the hellmouth.
Courtesy Bibliothèque Nationale, Paris

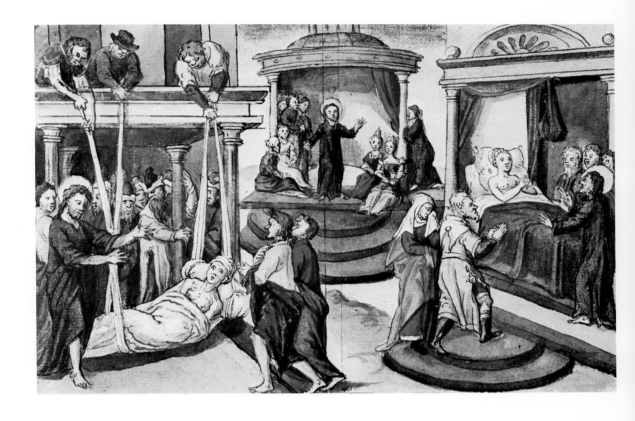

Figure 37
Scene from the Valenciennes passion play showing
the simultaneous depiction of several scenes. *Left,*
Christ curing the paralytic; *right,* Christ curing a
woman with dropsy. Courtesy Bibliothèque Nationale,
Paris

combined everyday dress overlaid with accessories that inspired awe and reverence for the heavenly figures, fear and terror for the figures of hell. When saints and important biblical personages appeared, they usually carried a specific symbol associated with them, such as Saint Peter carrying the keys. Only the common man appeared in plain everyday dress—a representative of man in medieval society caught between the supernatural forces of good and evil.

In the later medieval period there were play forms other than mystery plays, which were limited to biblical subjects. The most important of these were the miracle plays, about the lives of the saints; morality plays, such as the famous *Everyman;* and secular farces, such as *Master Pierre Pathelin.* All were short and included only one or two major incidents, and are more important for a study of the transition from the late Gothic to the early Renaissance than they are for an understanding of medieval thought and culture.

Of the mystery cycle playlets probably the most widely known is *The Second Shepherd's Play* from the Wakefield cycle of English mystery plays. It is the thirteenth play in a group of thirty-two short playlets that dramatized biblical events from the Creation to the Last Judgment. The plays in the Wakefield cycle were arranged and dramatized to create the simple linear progression found in illuminated medieval manuscripts. In *The Second Shepherd's Play,* which was based on the simple statement in Luke about the shepherds who watched over their flocks by night when the birth of the Lord was announced, the author has enriched this moment with comic detail, farcical humor, and a strong feeling for medieval peasant life. The juxtaposition of supernatural spirituality and earthy farcical reality in the playlet typified the completely unselfconscious religious thought of the medieval peasant and vividly illustrated the duality of outlook in all medieval art.

The seven roles in the playlet were originally played by men; the actor who played Gil, the wife of Mak, the ne'er-do-well shepherd, doubled as the Virgin Mary at the end of the playlet. A doll was probably used for the Christ child. The other shepherds are effectively characterized as having little psychological depth, although each has one or two quite specific personal traits or problems. Their generosity in wanting to give a gift to Gil and Mak's supposed baby finally unmasks Mak as a thief. Mak is portrayed as a wily, henpecked rogue who must communicate one thing to the shepherds and another to the audience, all with expert comic timing. Gil is a clever and shrewish wife. The religious figures in the last scene of the playlet are presented as religious stereotypes without personality. There are several demands for song in the playlet so that all actors would have to be capable singers.

The dialogue in this playlet is very simple and naïve because of the persistent use of rhymed verse. Some of the lines, however, are beautifully phrased and unpretentious, and illuminate a scene or a character with minimum effort. The theme is man's basic sinfulness and need of a savior. The shepherds represent the community attitude of the audience, Mak represents the sinners who need to be saved, and the Christ child is the symbol of God come to man. The criticism that the play is composed of two separate parts, the long farcical introduction and the final nativity scene, can be removed by seeing the two parts as a demonstration of sinfulness followed by the possibility of redemption. There is also a neat parallel between the two parts of the story: the comic mother, father, and "child," and the holy mother, father, and child. In one case, the child is a real lamb, in the other, a symbolic lamb of God. The shepherds who present gifts in both parts of the playlet provide dramatic continuity.

The rhythm of this playlet is similar to the unrolling, linear rhythm seen in medieval art. Music can be used to highlight the action. The physical requirements are for fields, Mak's house, and a manger. The same mansion can probably be used for both Mak's house and the manger, as long as there is a change of curtain. The mansion would have required a curtain to hide Gil and Mak when they were not on stage, as well as a door, a cradle, and a bed. If the mansion was placed on a pageant wagon, it is logical to assume that it would have pulled up to another flat-bedded wagon or stationary platform that could then have served as the open fields. Costumes for Mak and the shepherds would have been simple, medieval peasant tunics and hose. Gil would have worn the skirt and blouse of a lower-class woman; only Mary and the angel would have required some richer symbolic garments.

In producing this playlet for a modern audience, an attempt should be made to approximate the vivid, personal, naïve, decorative reality achieved by the medieval craftsmen who first produced it. (Sometimes the same artisans who presented the medieval mystery plays also decorated the cathedrals, and one is continually struck by the theatrical nature of the carved scenes of the Nativity or the Last Judgment.) The difference between the size of characters and their background, between the reality of personality and the unreality of the compositional method used to tell the story should be carefully stressed to capture the duality of the worldly and the unworldly in these plays.

The lines, textures, and colors of Gothic art can be studied with great profit in preparation for a modern production of one of the mystery plays. Color could reflect either the chalky frescoes of Giotto or the bright, clear, undiluted colors of stained glass, illuminated manuscripts, or heraldry. Line might reflect either the simple lines of Giotto's frescoes or the fascinating linear arabesques of the International Gothic style, while texture, which is usually subordinate to line and color in Gothic art, could reflect the rough surface of stone, the soft texture of wool, the carved texture of wood, or the brilliant transparency of stained glass.

Since the most important visual idea in a medieval play was the unrolling processional progression with all scene locations visible at the same time, some arrangement should be made so that the open fields, Mak's house, and the manger are seen together, possibly using a single mansion or mansions set in an open space with a change of curtains for the Nativity scene. The mansion either could be a structural decorative Gothic framework for action, as in many manuscript illuminations or sculptural scenes, or it could suggest a specific space in miniature as in the paintings of Giotto (Fig. 38). If the play is going to be produced as part of a series of cycle dramas, then a decorative architectural frame-

Figure 38
Giotto. *Meeting of Joachim and Anna,* ca. 1305. An example of the use of a theatrical mansion to stage a scene from the Bible. Courtesy Alinari-Anderson, Florence

Figure 39
Shepherds in the Fields, Chartres Cathedral (royal
portal), early thirteenth century. An example of the
naïve simplicity and faith found in early Gothic
sculpture. Photo Jean Roubier, Paris

Figure 40
Scene from *The Second Shepherd's Play* from the
Wakefield cycle of mystery plays, produced at the
Parish Church, Stratford-upon-Avon, England, 1950,
under the direction of Henry Clark. Courtesy Henry
Clark.

work, which could be used for other productions, would be the best design choice.

Properties should obviously be kept realistic and simple, and costumes should be limited to the medieval peasant hoods, tunics, cloaks, and hose which are worn, for example, by the two shepherds in a section of the royal portal of the cathedral at Chartres (Fig. 39). Here we have an excellent example of the fit and drape of two simple, lower-class costumes that would be right for the play. The draping of the hoods, the wrinkles in the hose, the folds on the sleeves—all make a decorative linear statement that could be achieved in actual costume by the correct choice of soft woolens and the right cutting and fitting of the garments. The Virgin Mary and the angel should be clothed in the religiously symbolic colors and garments found in illuminated manuscripts, statues, and paintings of the Gothic period. A balance of simplicity and casual beauty can be admirably adapted to the costumes for the shepherds in this play to bring together the naïve charm of the opening scenes, the farcical humor of the middle scenes, and the religious beauty of the final tableau (Fig. 40).

3

Renaissance Theatre

Traditionally the Renaissance is said to have begun in Florence at the beginning of the fifteenth century as a reaction to the overwrought decorative flamboyance of late Gothic styles in art and a rediscovery of the art and ideas of antiquity. Historians and philosophers of the late nineteenth and early twentieth centuries saw the culmination of this reaction and rediscovery in a short but brilliant period labeled the High Renaissance. This period, dominated by geniuses like Michelangelo, Leonardo da Vinci, and Raphael, was thought to have been followed by a century of decadence and decline, illuminated with moments of brilliance supplied by such writers as Cervantes and Shakespeare. This is now considered an oversimplified view, and the years between 1400 and 1600 are now divided into three distinct artistic periods.

First, a period that drew to a close about 1490 was dominated by experimentation and analysis of all aspects of the human and natural world. Although humanism and naturalism were not totally new concepts discovered by fifteenth century artists, a new objectivity and scientific approach did triumph during these years. The beautiful, curving lines and flat, decorative patterns of the International Gothic style were

succeeded by the tactile forms, mathematical precision, simple dignity, and compact unity of artists like Masaccio, Donatello, Brunelleschi, and their followers (Fig. 41). The new art was for the most part neither metaphysical, symbolic, romantic, nor ceremonial; it stood as a method for later fifteenth century artists to analyze and dissect.

Second, the period known as the High Renaissance, which lasted roughly from the last decade of the fifteenth century until the death of Raphael in 1520, is no longer seen only as the culmination and integration of artistic forces that were developing in Italy since the time of Giotto, but as a period of innovation led by artists who were given great scope by the Church under the powerful and worldly popes Alexander VI, Julius II, and Leo X. The works of Michelangelo, Raphael, Leonardo da Vinci, and Bramante, which in some ways represented the culimination of artistic experiments of the fifteenth century, were also new in their scope, breadth of outlook, complexity, size, and ideal beauty. This new artistic ideal stemmed in great part from the outlooks and patronage of towering authority figures determined to establish Rome as the seat of grandeur and power for the Catholic Church (Fig. 42).

Third, the years following the death of Raphael are seen today not as a decline in art but as a move toward more personal and less natural interpretations of reality—the so-called *desegno interno* based on the inner personality and outlook of the individual artist. The optimism of the early and High Renaissance waned with the invasions of Italy in the early sixteenth century, the rise of the Reformation, and the final horror of the sack of Rome in 1527. The resultant malaise and disillusionment turned artists inward and away from nature, and led to artistic mannerisms that deliberately distorted and exaggerated many of the artistic ideals of the Renaissance and created disturbing psychological effects for the viewer (Fig. 43). This art, known as mannerism, spread to the rest of Europe in the first half of the sixteenth century, and the artists and writers of England, France, Germany, and Spain naturally incorporated into their work a mixture of Renaissance precepts and mannerist

Figure 41
Donatello. *David,* ca. 1430–1432. The first life-sized,
fully free-standing Renaissance nude statue. Courtesy
Alinari, Florence

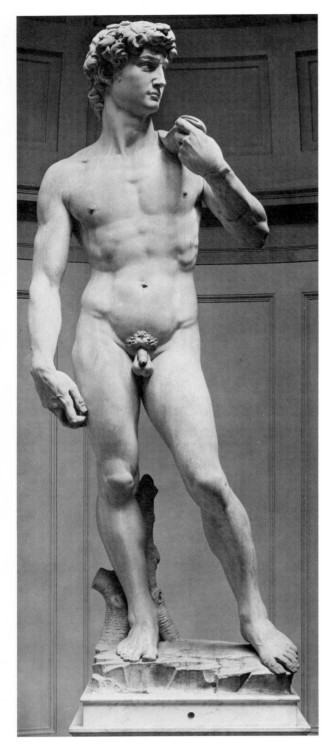

Figure 42
Michelangelo. *David*, 1501–1504. An example of the
heroic scale, monumental grandeur, and unified
emotional power of the High Renaissance. Courtesy
Alinari, Florence

Figure 43
Tintoretto. *The Last Supper,* 1592–1594. An exaggerated perspective, a brilliant night light, and a
self-consciously choreographed action create a sense
of mystery and theatricality in the works of Tintoretto, El Greco, and other late sixteenth century
mannerists. Courtesy Alinari, Florence

interpretations. The Italian artists who moved north and west after 1520 were only nominally Renaissance artists; psychologically they were mannerists, creating and teaching an art that was personal, distorted, ambiguous, and unnatural. Mannerist art sifted into England late in the reign of Henry VIII and conditioned the artistic and cultural setting in which Shakespeare developed.

Before we discuss the stylistic relationship between Shakespeare and the various artistic trends that made up the two centuries of the Renaissance, something should be said about the two threads of theatrical development in Italy that eventually had at least a peripheral influence on Shakespeare. With the revival of interest in antiquity in the fifteenth century, an interest in Greek and Roman theatre developed (even Shakespeare mirrors this interest in plays like *Julius Caesar* and *Antony and Cleopatra*). By the early sixteenth century, every prince or duke who prided himself on his taste for ancient culture had classical plays and entertainments produced at his court. The staging of these productions stemmed from two traditions: one that emulated the permanent theater background of the Roman theater (based on the drawings and discussions in the architectural treatise written by the Roman architect Vitruvius), and one that derived from the contemporary fascination with perspective painting. These two traditions finally came together in the first permanent Italian Renaissance theater, the Teatro Olimpico at Vicenza, designed by Andrea Palladio and opened in 1585 (Fig. 44). The plan for the Teatro Olimpico followed Vitruvius quite closely, but the influence of perspective painting is very evident in the alleyways designed in sloped perspective behind the five doors of the proscenium façade. Although Shakespeare's stage could make little use of perspective scenery because of the seating arrangements in Elizabethan theaters, it is possible that the large central door of the Teatro Olimpico influenced the use of the central pavilion to frame important scenes in the Elizabethan theater.

A more important thread of theatrical development that influenced

Figure 44
The stage of the Teatro Olimpico at Vicenza with Scamozzi's added perspective vistas (*above*) and Palladio's *scaenae frons* (*below*), late sixteenth century. An example of both the strong interest in the theatre of classical antiquity and the Renaissance preoccupation with perspective. Courtesy Norman Philbrick Library

Teatro di Vicenza del Palladio

Scala di
5 10 20 30 40 50 60 70 80 90 100   Palmi Romani

Razullo.   Cucurucu.

Renaissance Theatre

72

Shakespeare's playwriting was the commedia dell'arte, which developed in Italy during the sixteenth through eighteenth centuries. Groups of itinerant professional actors, none of whom were aristocrats with education and courtly manners, toured the countryside and, on an open wooden platform in the marketplace, improvised comedies based on stock characters—lovers, the miserly merchant (the Pantalone); the long-winded schoolmaster (the Dottore); the cowardly but boasting soldier (the Capitano); and a number of roguish comic servants called *Zanni*. All characters but the lovers wore masks and traditional costumes, and in many ways they all reflected character types from Roman comedy and farce (Fig. 45). The actors developed set speeches as well as clever bits of business, known as *lazzi*, which were used to spark audience interest whenever the plot or action began to lag.

This popular comic style, which spread to all of Europe by the close of the sixteenth century, appears to have influenced Shakespeare when he wrote *The Taming of the Shrew* and *Henry IV*, parts 1 and 2, where the character of Falstaff is clearly related to the Capitano (Fig. 46).

With the knowledge we have today of the changing artistic and cultural styles in the sixteenth century, we can no longer view Shakespeare as the great Renaissance humanist-romantic whose works have been traditionally considered to represent a single artistic perspective, except for certain so-called inferior plays. Endowed with great powers of observation and compassionate humanism, Shakespeare managed to absorb and reflect in some twenty years of work the entire range of movements and forces prevailing in England from the fifteenth to the early seventeenth century. This was possible particularly in England because the country was emerging from a belated medieval past at the same time it was absorbing the complex ideas of the Renaissance and mannerism. Unlike other European countries, where this development took at least a century, England, from the defeat of the Armada through the early years of the reign of James I, was a crossroads and a meeting ground for more than a century of European cultural ideals.

Figure 45
Jacques Callot. Sketch of two figures from the commedia dell'arte, ca. 1620. Callot's sketches of Italian comedy figures vividly capture the gay, exuberant crudity of early seventeenth century Italian popular theatre. Courtesy National Gallery of Art, Washington, D.C., Rosenwald Collection

Renaissance Theatre

74

Although Shakespeare's works did not follow a simple pattern of development, they did follow roughly the progressive cultural developments of England. Shakespeare's earliest plays were medieval in organizational structure and subject matter, his early comedies reflected the youth of Renaissance European culture and its optimism and exuberant simplicity, and his mature works were marked by the probing, personal, inward unrest and ambiguities that we associate with mannerism. In his very last plays there was even a stress on the visual richness and the idea of climax and reconciliation that we associate with the thought and art of the Baroque period.

A word should be said about the nature of Shakespeare's theatre and the strengths and limitations it created for his work. The dramas that developed first in amateur production and later in the professional outdoor playhouses after 1576 were a curious mixture of native medieval interludes and folk tales, with an injection of the new classical learning. There was a wide range of subject matter and approach, and Shakespeare inherited few strong limitations of storytelling method other than those created by the physical theater for which he wrote. The Elizabethan playhouse was either round, square, or polygonal and held approximately 2,500 spectators who either stood in the central yard or pit or sat in the surrounding roofed balconies. The stage, a raised platform projecting midway into the yard, was partially covered by a roof or "heaven" supported by pillars, and backed by either a wall with doors or a curtained inner stage flanked by large doors. An upper stage, frequently used by Shakespeare, was an important second acting level. Scholars have not established whether the inner and upper stages were permanent features of the theater or whether they were created as special pavilions for specific productions and placed against the balcony and back wall of the stage. A curtained inner stage is needed for discovering actors at the beginning of a scene in many Shakespearean plays. Windows above the stage doors were probably used for certain scenes. A

Figure 46
A scene from the American Conservatory Theatre's 1974 production of *The Taming of the Shrew*, directed by Bill Ball, designed by Robert Fletcher. An example of the direct application of commedia dell'arte costumes and techniques to Shakespearean comedy. Courtesy William Ganslen, photographer, San Francisco, California

Figure 47
Johann de Witt. Drawing of the Swan Theatre, London, 1596. The only contemporary drawing of the Elizabethan stage showing a partially covered platform projecting into the yard, surrounded by balconies of spectators, and backed by two doors and a stage balcony. From Johann de Witt's sketch as copied by Arend van Buchell

Figure 48
A sketch from a production of *Titus Andronicus*, 1595. An example of the mixture of contemporary and classical dress on the Elizabethan stage. From the original drawing in the possession of the Marquess of Bath

third level for musicians could sometimes be used for supernatural appearances (Fig. 47).

The lists of theatre businessman Philip Henslowe give us some idea of the minimal scenery used on the Elizabethan stage: rocks, trees, furniture, hellmouths, and a back-cloth representing Rome. Machinery housed below stage brought ghosts through trap doors in the floor; ropes and pullies raised objects and people to the upper stage. Fire and smoke, the sound of cannons, bells, thunder, and other effects could be produced.

Lighting was unnecessary because performances were by daylight, but torches, candles, and lanterns were used to indicate night. Costumes were of two kinds: the symbolic and the contemporary. The symbolic costumes, which represented gods, supernatural beings, animals, foreign figures, and servants, were usually made specifically for the company wardrobe; the contemporary costumes, worn by the majority of the characters in a production, were usually donated by the noblemen who sponsored the company (Fig. 48). The company was usually composed of ten to twenty members, some of them shareholders who shared in a

Renaissance Theatre

78

percentage of the profits, while the others were hired at a fixed fee. Young boy apprentices played the female roles, and extras or supers were taken on for individual productions. The audience was composed of all levels of society, from the nobility in the balcony and on the edges of the stage to the "groundlings" who stood in the yard.

Romeo and Juliet, one of Shakespeare's early plays, portrays the playwright's instinctive understanding of early Renaissance spirit and artistic organization. There is a directness, a lightness, a delicacy, and charm that match the youthfulness of the early Renaissance artistic outlook, and there is a stress on symmetry and balance.

When we look at the structural pattern of *Romeo and Juliet*, we are immediately struck by the obvious symmetrical layout of the foreground figures against a background of town squares, orchards, and rooms that suggest the horizontal recessional planes of fifteenth century Italian art. Figures and events tend to group themselves like those in a Ghiberti panel or a Botticelli painting (Fig. 49). Take the matter of the feud, for example: in the opening scene, at the banishment, and at the close of the play the balance of opposing enmities is given central focus in the figure of the Prince of Verona, who, standing above the quarrel, divides Capulet from Montague.

The characters are neatly balanced against one another: Romeo against Paris and Mercutio, Juliet against Rosaline, the Nurse against Lady Capulet, Capulet against Montague. All the players are arranged on three levels of recession into the background: Romeo and Juliet stand out sharply in front of the Nurse, Friar Laurence, and Mercutio, the group of middle ground characters, while Tybalt, the Capulets, Paris, and Benvolio are two-dimensional background characters.

The ideas of the play are a compound of opposites: love and hate, rashness and caution, courtly love and passionate love, tolerance and intolerance, purity and sensuality, night and day, sleep and death. The theme of star-crossed lovers is kept ever in the foreground, triumphing over the evil and tragedy that result from the feud between the two families. Shakespeare relied heavily on the tightly balanced form of the

Figure 49
Botticelli. *The Adoration of the Kings*, ca. 1478. An example of a scene composed in a frontal plane of balanced symmetry and rich simplicity that relates to the compositional method in *Romeo and Juliet*.
Courtesy Alinari, Florence

sonnet, and the language of the play is rich in poetic set pieces that can be lifted out and looked at separately. There is in the play's language a certain symmetry and polished beauty as well as the lightness and sparkle of youth.

The rhythmic mood of the piece makes a major change from lightness at the opening to heaviness at the close, from the measured pace of the earlier scenes to the breathless rush to the conclusion. Time is the villain and Shakespeare used every rhythmic device to make haste and speed the very essence of the play's tragedy. The scenes of the play come vividly to life because each seems a clearly marked-off, boxed-in space. Thus, even on an Elizabethan stage, the scenes can be placed clearly and securely as localized areas connected by horizontal movement: the upper stage for the bedchamber, the window for the balcony scene, the inner stage for the tomb, and on both sides of the stage, the doors that house the retainers of the two families.

In staging the play, the very localized nature of each scene may lead a director to choose a series of enclosed box sets, as Zeffirelli did in his famous production of 1960, but such a choice detracts from the speed and haste of the play's rhythm. A method must be devised that gives both speed of action and a clearly defined sense of separate areas of stage space. The basic spaces of the Elizabethan stage will work, and in one respect they are almost essential: the dramatic irony of Juliet's "death" after the potion scene is not fully absorbed unless her body, laid out on the bed, is fully visible above the action of the subsequent scenes, which involve the arrival of the musicians, the flowers, and the richly dressed wedding figure of the County Paris. Steps, doors, windows, and platforms can usually be arranged to provide an upper area for the bedroom and the balcony, a raised area for the Prince, side doors or arches leading into the central square, a large area for the ballroom, and a small forward area for Friar Lawrence's cell. Within such an ar-

Figure 50
Mary Anderson as Juliet and Mrs. Sterling as the nurse in an 1887 production of *Romeo and Juliet.* An excellent example of the detailed use of Victorian fabric textures and trim in a Renaissance play. Costume lines were strongly influenced by the correct ideas of fashion in the historical productions of the late nineteenth century. Photo from Gebbie and Gebbie, *The Stage and Its Stars,* vol. 1. Courtesy Norman Philbrick Library

81

rangement (which should involve minimal changes during the action) the designer will want to suggest the symmetrical forms, the simplicity of line and ornament, and the brightness of color that we associate with the early Renaissance. Even if a period other than the early Renaissance is chosen as a setting for the play, these abstract qualities that are so much a part of the play can be used. For example, if the play is set in the 1590s, when it was written, the twisted complexities and grotesque ambiguities of late sixteenth century mannerist art should be interpreted appropriately to emphasize the symmetry and simplicity of the early Renaissance.

The most natural period to use in a production of *Romeo and Juliet* is the Italian Renaissance. If another period is chosen, however, the choices in line, texture, and color should reflect the abstract qualities found in fifteenth century Italian painting. If the play is set in the Elizabethan period, the designer must work diligently to lighten the mannerist costume lines, remove the heavy decoration, and avoid the stiffening and underpinning that would falsify the inner structure and nature of the play. The same is true of a heavy-handed romantic approach. Although such an approach was quite usual in the nineteenth century, it went against the direct, light, symmetrical nature of the play (Fig. 50). Rich brocades should be put aside in favor of soft, supple fabrics, with an emphasis on the beauty of draping rather than the heavy complex surfaces. Fabrics with a soft or even a crisp sheen, and accented with transparencies such as we find in the paintings of Botticelli, are far better than cut velvets and heavy velours. Simple lines that show off the human figure are more appropriate than complex, body-distorting fashion lines, and the light blonde colors of a Botticelli painting are superior to the rich tones of a Titian painting. *Romeo and Juliet* is both a play of youth and a youthful play and it partakes in its nature of the youth of Renaissance culture.

Hamlet, written only a handful of years after *Romeo and Juliet,* partakes of the maturity and world-weariness of European Renaissance culture. With the disillusionment and despair that followed the Essex Rebellion,

England began to turn into a police state, and the high spirits that had followed the defeat of the Armada gradually gave way to Jacobean gloom and malaise. England had long used mannerist ideals in a decorative, ornamental way, but now began to accept the disturbed art of mannerism as an expression of the social and psychological disturbances of the time. Hamlet, with a tainted mind and a heavy heart, and obsessed by an almost medieval sense of death, resides in this new world and contemplates the rottenness of the state.

When we look at the structure of the play, we find a very complex web of inner and outer realities and a continuous shift of the action from foreground soliloquy to background pageantry that leaves the audience with a sense of ambiguity and disturbance. The forces of the play seem violently driven, overly dramatic, and deeply ironic. As in much mannerist art, Hamlet operates both within and without the action, presenting the story in a way that is analogous to the gesturing figure frequently used by Tintoretto and El Greco (see Figs. 43 and 51).

Characterization in this play is ambiguous, primarily because of Hamlet, whose shifts in temperament are extreme and even neurotic. Hamlet's character develops from opposing impulses; the only discernible line of development is that toward death, from the "To be or not to be" speech to the "Readiness is all" speech. We are never certain of how much Hamlet is playacting and how much he deeply senses the existential nothingness of life. The other characters are used to provide contrast to Hamlet and to demonstrate some aspect of the ill health of the state. All the characters act indirectly, all have biases or only partial views of the facts, and all help to define the action.

In many ways the themes of this play remind us of the themes of Sophocles' *Oedipus Rex.* Both plays begin with an invocation for the well-being of the state; in both, the destiny of an individual and a society is closely intertwined, and the suffering of a royal victim seems necessary before purgation and renewal can take place. The theme of order within the Renaissance monarchy is similar to the theme of order within the Greek cosmos.

The language of *Hamlet* is immensely complex, composed of broken rhythms, abrupt contrasts, and a heavy stress on the creation of strong sensory imagery. Words such as *blasted, mildewed, apoplexe'd, ulcerous, tumour, infect, corruption, rank, smell* vividly conjure up images of sickness. Throughout the play the language is used in a changing, shifting way to build very complicated pictorial images of life.

The rhythmic movement of the play is also sharply shifting, as it moves from soft, quiet speeches to high-pitched hysterical ones, from slow movement to rapid movement. The rhythm moves from the tensions in a coiled spring to the moments of relaxation in a slowly moving stream, and the audience never knows what rhythmic pattern will come next.

The three great opportunities for visual splendor are the opening court scene, the court scene in which the play is presented, and the final court scene in which the duel takes place. These ritual-ceremonial scenes, representing the social order of the decaying state, demand full pageantry, and, far more than the smaller, intimate scenes, should reflect in their spatial arrangements the rhythms and structural composition of the play.

In presenting the play today, the first choice a designer must make is whether to use some approximation of Elizabethan stage locations or to create some other multiple-area arrangement of stage space. Having the upper stage for the parapet, the trap doors for the grave, the full width from door to door for the large court scenes, and the forestage for soliloquies has its advantages, but it also has its disadvantages: there is a certain rigidity and lack of rhythmic flow from area to area if the stage space is not specifically designed to match the structural rhythm. The best solution is to keep those elements of the Elizabethan stage that further the rhythmic flow of the action and incorporate them into a stage plan that will emphasize the mannerist compositional tensions of the script.

The arrangement of space for the three court scenes is crucial. Particularly for the court scene in which the play is presented, the director must decide if the audience is to look through the backs of the king and

Figure 51
El Greco. *The Burial of Count Orgaz,* 1586. A famous mannerist painting that could be used as an inspiration for a production of *Hamlet.* Courtesy D. P. Dominguez-Parocco and the Spanish National Tourist Office

queen to the players, glance at them on the side of the stage while they watch the play, or observe the players performing downstage in front of Claudius and Gertrude. The mannerist qualities in the play's structure can be brought out most successfully by an asymmetrical, somewhat unstable placement of colors that will give a sense of imbalance and discomfort to the scene. The same will be true if there is an asymmetrical placement of the thrones in the three court scenes. In each scene, the way in which the throne is placed is very important in creating the appropriate sense of instability in the action, which can be further emphasized at times of crisis by the use of diagonal and recessional movement of the actors. At the close of the action, when Fortinbras arrives, an upstage center entrance is needed to return the play to symmetrical calm and stability.

The tilted composition, sharp shifts in focus, and strong eruptions of artificial light in Tintoretto's *The Last Supper* might be read as a visual analogy for much of the compositional method in *Hamlet* (see Fig. 43). Although the painting cannot be used in a literal way as a design source for the play, it can serve as a creative stimulus to the imagination and a visual catalyst for the images and impressions suggested by the script. For example, the sulfurous, torch-lit illumination of the painting reminds one of that moment in *Hamlet* when Claudius rushes from the scene calling for lights. A designer, in choosing textures and colors for *Hamlet,* might borrow heavily from *The Last Supper* to create the appropriate mood in the ceremonial court scenes. Another mannerist painting, *The Burial of Count Orgaz* by El Greco might be used as a visual inspiration for a set of costumes for *Hamlet* (see Fig. 51). The sulfurous yellows, heavy golds, acid greens, and harsh magentas against background accents of black, white, and gray convey a sense of theatricality, uneasiness, and mystery that is further enhanced by the contrast between the crackling light on certain fabric folds and the heavy immobility of the great gold robes. Hamlet might be dressed in black, like the boy in the left foreground who seems to introduce the drama, while Claudius and Gertrude

Figure 52
Caspar David Friedrich. *Man and Wife Gazing at the Moon,* 1819. An example of the tight technique and melancholy mood found in the works of the German romantic painters. Courtesy Nationalgalerie, Berlin

might wear the rich, overlarge, brocaded gold robes of the church fathers as symbols of the power of the state. The costumes of the Player King and Queen might reflect in exaggerated and distorted patterns of black and white the royal gowns of Claudius and Gertrude, and the costumes of Polonius, Rosencrantz, and Guildenstern might be accented with magenta, yellow, or green. The armor of the dead count can be used for the ghost, the noblemen dressed in black for the court personages, and the robes worn by the Jesuit priests for ominous accents in all large, ceremonial scenes.

Both Tintoretto and El Greco were contemporaries of Shakespeare. A German romantic painter of the early nineteenth century with many mannerist tendencies, such as Caspar David Friedrich, could also be used as inspiration for a production set in the 1820s (Fig. 52). Friedrich's lonely figures silhouetted in the moonlight in front of gnarled trees, misty harbors, and open windows create a sense of mystery, pessimism, and melancholy that would be very appropriate for a production of *Hamlet* that stressed the romantic and melancholy aspects of Hamlet's character (Fig. 53).

In a production of *Hamlet,* the measure of success is not in the novelty of the production but in the sensitivity with which space, fabrics, colors, and ornament are integrated into the appropriate visual and rhythmic support for the play's action (Fig. 54).

Figure 53
Costume design by the author for Claudius in a production of *Hamlet,* presented by the Stanford Players, Stanford University, 1963. The production, set in the German romantic period of 1820, stressed the dark and the melancholy aspects of the play. From the collection of the author

Figure 54
A scene from *Hamlet,* presented by the Royal Shakespeare Company of Stratford-on-Avon and London in 1966 under the direction of Peter Hall. Designed by John Bury. Courtesy the Royal Shakespeare Company. Photo by Reg Wilson

4

Baroque Theatre

It is often difficult for a designer to know what approach to use in modern theatre productions of the tragedies of Racine or the less perfected imitations of Dryden. Should they be done in classical dress, in seventeenth century stage costume, or in abstract or simplified contemporary dress? There is no single answer for any one production, but a close analysis of both Baroque culture and the structure of a particular play can provide many secure guidelines for production.

The opening of the seventeenth century saw a reaffirmation of the power of the Catholic Church as well as an expansion of Protestant confidence, and the doubts, insecurities, and tensions of mannerist sixteenth century culture were gradually left behind. Part of the new wholeness of outlook and universality of vision may also be attributed to the new view of man and his universe, which stemmed from the discoveries of Copernicus, Galileo, and Kepler. With the theory that the earth moved about the sun instead of being the center of the universe, the cosmos came to be seen as an infinite continuity of interrelationships that embraced even man in its unbroken and systematic whole. The new elliptical patterns of movement established for heavenly bodies had a direct

effect on compositional patterns in art. The exaggerated effects, the lighting from within or from the beyond, and the movement leading outside the frame of a work of art can be viewed as expressions of a striving after the infinite. Just as Gothic art strove to suggest the spiritual, so Baroque art strove to suggest the infinite.

The Baroque is a complex style, which we usually think of as operatic, sensuous, flamboyant, and terribly grand. Yet this is only one aspect of the style—the Baroque we associate with opera, grand ceiling paintings, and expansive Austrian and Italian architectural designs. The style differed sharply from country to country, from north to south, from Catholic areas to Protestant, and from the early to the late seventeenth century. Roughly and very imprecisely, the Baroque can be divided into three artistic styles: operatic baroque, classic baroque, and baroque realism.

Operatic or flamboyant baroque art originated in courtly and Catholic areas. This was the art of Bernini and Rubens and the new form of opera, aimed at supporting and enhancing the grandeur and absolute power of secular rulers and princes of the Church. The style was characterized by a richness of materials, a sense of excitement, movement, and energy, an illusion of great depth and space, and a theatrical and concentrated use of lighting. The style began in Italy and Flanders at the beginning of the seventeenth century in the work of Bernini, Rubens, and other painters and architects, and spread to Austria, southern Germany, and all of Italy during the later part of the century (Fig. 55).

The classical baroque style developed in Italy also at the beginning of the seventeenth century in the work of the Carracci brothers, Agostino and Annibale, and was carried from Italy to France by Poussin and his many followers during the years that saw the founding of the French Academy. This style placed strong emphasis on the study of the classical artists of the Renaissance as well as of antiquity, and further developed the concept of decorum, where every aspect of a work of art was appropriate without excess or overstatement. The subject matter of such

Figure 55
Bernini. *Apollo and Daphne,* 1622–1625. An example of an integrated sculptural group that captures an exact moment in the drama taken from Ovid's *Metamorphoses.* Courtesy Alinari, Florence

Baroque Theatre

94

work was based on mythology or Greek, Roman, and biblical history. There was great stress on elevated style, and individual aspects of nature and personality were subordinated to the ideal of the regular and the universal. It is this art that one must study in its various manifestations in France during the reign of Louis XIV to understand the art of both Molière and Racine (Fig. 56).

The baroque realism of Velásquez, Rembrandt, Caravaggio, and many other painters was opposed to grandiose subject matter and large-scale compositions, and stressed closely focused lower-class or genre subjects treated with great individuality, personality, and detail. Historical and biblical events were also treated as genre subjects (Fig. 57). Theatrical lighting from a single source was brilliantly manipulated for dramatic effect. The style developed in Italy under Caravaggio, was carried to Holland by a group of artists who influenced Rembrandt, and spread to Spain by way of southern Italy. It is a style that came to Molière through his study of the commedia dell'arte.

The actual physical theater during the Baroque period gradually became a picture-frame stage built to house the grandeurs of opera. The auditorium was usually a U-shaped structure lined with tiers of boxes, sometimes with a gallery above the top row of boxes at the rear of the theater for servants and apprentices. Sight lines from the side boxes were poor, and the flat floor area usually held only standees (at least half-way back into the auditorium to where benches were sometimes placed). The deep stage was raked upward and framed by an ornate proscenium arch. There was considerable space below the stage for machinery and trap doors, space above for hanging sky borders, and space on the sides for the side wings to move out of sight behind the proscenium. Lighting generally came from chandeliers hung in the auditorium and over the stage, from footlights set behind reflectors along the stage edge, or from lights set against reflectors behind each set of wings. The wings moved in grooves on the stage and in each group there were as many wings as there were locations in the production. Two large flats

Figure 56
Poussin. *Holy Family on the Steps,* ca. 1656. An example of the elevated style and decorum of the classical Baroque. Courtesy National Gallery of Art, Washington, D.C., Samuel H. Kress Collection

Baroque Theatre

96

or shutters that met in the center formed the back wall, and there were as many of these as the scenes in the play or the opera required. At each change of scene, a set of shutters, wings, and borders were drawn away from the stage, in full view of the audience, to reveal the next set in place.

Costumes for the operas and classical tragedies produced within these settings were rich, ornamental, formalized garments based on a combination of contemporary garments and certain items from classical antiquity. A plumed helmet or headdress, a breastplate-shaped tunic, a skirt flared to above the knee, a mantle, and short, soft, calf-high boots completed the standard costume for men, although long robes were worn by older or special characters. The costume for women usually consisted of a court gown with a hip-length overskirt, and labels or tabs at the edge of the overskirt, the waist, the collar, and the shoulders. Sleeves were usually full and caught back to the elbow, and the hair or headdress was adorned with plumes. From this basic structure ingenious designers were able to develop variations to suggest Turks, Indians, and mythological beasts (Fig. 58). In the comedies of Molière and the playwrights of the Restoration, the costume style was basically contemporary dress accented by exaggerated effects for comic comment. The important point for the modern designer to understand is that no matter how overlaid with decoration and ornament a costume was in this period, it was based on a very carefully balanced structure, just as the basic structure of Baroque architecture was carefully organized before rich ornament was added.

The style of the operatic baroque is useful for developing designs for operas of the seventeenth century, while the style of the classical baroque, particularly the work of Poussin, is useful for developing a visual approach to Racine. Take, for example, Racine's greatest tragedy, *Phèdre*, a perfect example of a tragedy of reason based on a single moment of experience and a single angle of vision. Racine followed with great fidelity the rules for tragedy developed by the neoclassical theorists after the Renaissance. In structure he followed the overly strict interpretation

Figure 57
Velásquez. *Christ and the Pilgrims of Emmaus,* ca. 1625–1630. An example of close focus on a small group lit by artificial light that characterized baroque realism. Courtesy The Metropolitan Museum of Art. Bequest of Benjamin Altman, 1913

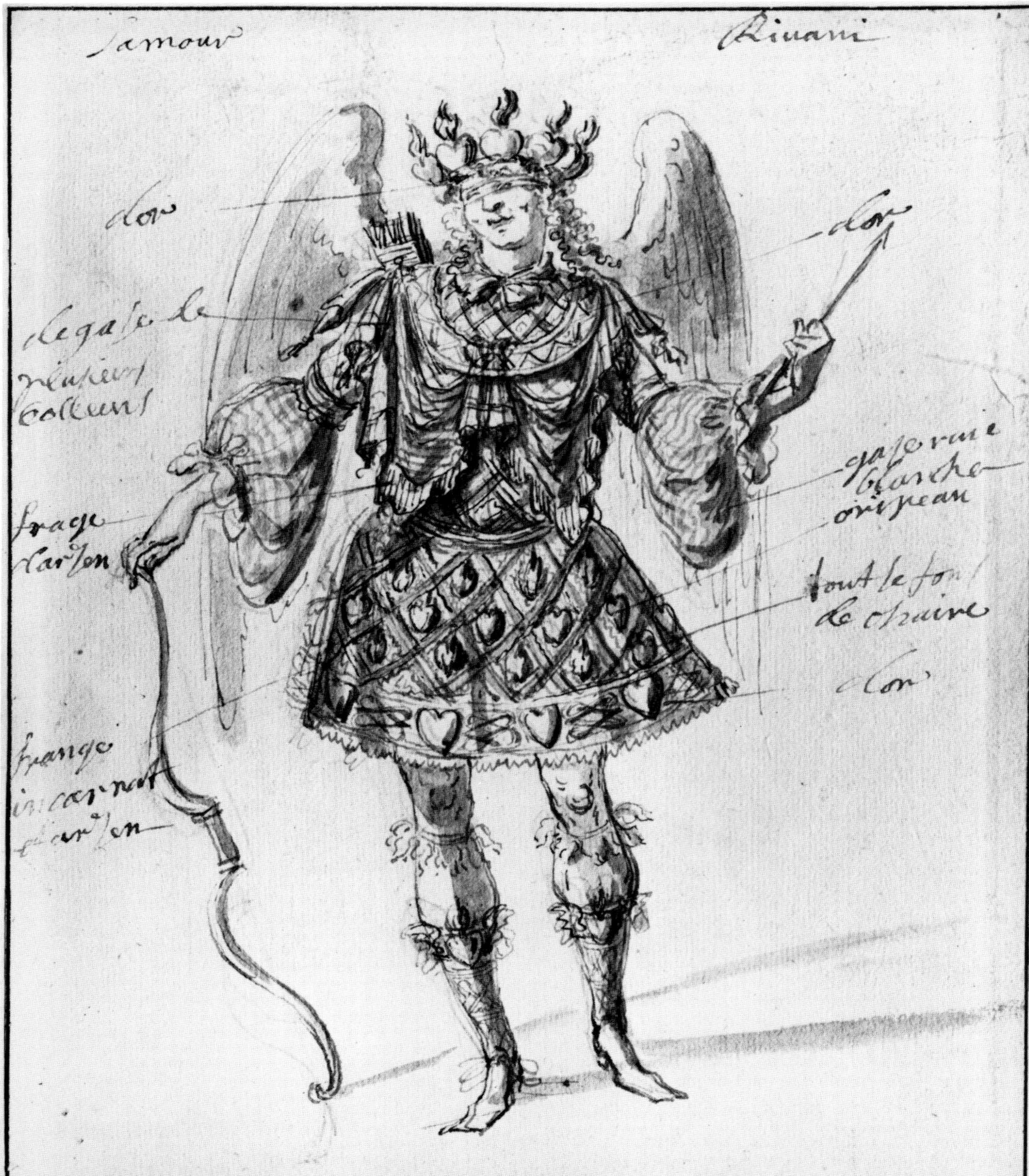

of Aristotle that demanded a singleness of action developed in a single place during a single day, and he interpreted the word *action* to mean the psychological results of action, not its physical events on the stage. Thus, the external action in the *Phèdre* is very simple, while the psychological action and character relationships are very complex.

In refashioning Euripides' *Hippolytus* for his seventeenth century *Phèdre,* Racine eliminated the chorus, reduced the importance of the gods in relation to human action, and substituted for the natural, religious world view of the Greeks a limited, artificial ritual based on the strategies and rules found at the court of Louis XIV. Although there was a greatly diminished sense of man in relation to nature, there was an increased stress on rational perfection and polished organization in the play's structure.

Racine was a master of psychological characterization, particularly of the female personality. The shifts in Phèdre's moods and the subtle changes in her emotions must be presented sharply through a great range of histrionic ability, yet the smallest nuances of emotional change must not be lost. This psychological subtlety is embedded in a tight structural form in which all the characters attempt to act rationally and are then swayed by irrational forces that seem beyond their control, and all are drawn according to the character rules of neoclassicism, that is, they are of noble birth, they act with dignity and decorum, and they abide by the rules of personal honor.

The theme of the *Phèdre,* like the themes in the historical, biblical, and mythological paintings of Poussin, is that duty, honor, and a strong sense of personal integrity must triumph over passion, and that tragedy results when passion is allowed to usurp the need for reason, decorum, and good breeding in society. Racine communicated this theme in language controlled by the rigidities of the French alexandrine, which, within twelve-foot lines, can build to great, towering climaxes and then ebb to devastating quietness. Such great speeches or "tirades," when brilliantly performed, can bring an audience to its feet in tumultuous

Figure 58
Design for a theatrical costume by Henri Gissey, from an original drawing in the Victoria and Albert Museum, second half of the seventeenth century. Courtesy Victoria and Albert Museum, Crown Copyright

applause; all actors who have performed in this drama agree that to do justice to the language takes tremendous vocal technique and emotional control.

The tragic rhythm of the drama derives directly from the ebb and flow of the carefully ordered verse form of the French alexandrine, and since there are no abrupt breaks in the action, the progression throughout the play is as clear and inexorable as the rhythm of the sea.

Racine indicated nothing concrete about the physical presentation of the tragedy, except that the play takes place in the Palace of Troezen. In the original presentation, furnishings must have been minimal or nonexistent, the setting simple, symmetrical, grand, and monumental; the costumes would have reflected the station and inherent decorum of each character, and the lighting was probably constant. The problem for the designer of a modern revival of *Phèdre* is whether to go to Greek sources for setting and costumes, to create a modern adaptation of seventeenth century staging methods, or to do the whole play in abstract modern dress. Although it may seem most logical to go to Greek sources because of the nature of the characters and the story, this is probably least helpful to the mood and structure of the drama. If this choice is made, however, then the designer should go not only to Greek sources, but also to the paintings of Racine's contemporary, Poussin, who, like Racine, set out to distill earlier baroque excesses into essences of emotion and thought conceived of and organized in a rational manner. It is not the garments and the settings themselves that should be studied in the paintings of Poussin, but the use of shapes, lines, colors, balance, and proportion. Having studied these aspects, the designer can apply them to Greek sources and produce a drama that combines Greek settings with the cool, heroic, artificial, artistic effects found in the works of Poussin and Racine (Fig. 59).

Greek draperies of the fifth century B. C., however, even when interpreted "à la Poussin," cannot capture the formality, decorum, and artificiality of the French court reflected in this play. Only seventeenth

Figure 59
A scene from *Phèdre* by Racine, produced by the University of Kansas City in 1958, with costumes by the author. A few strong, clear colors were used throughout. Gowns were of thick, wide-wale corduroy, breastplates were of felt, and trim was of heavy, gold braid. Photo by author

Phedre

Theseus

century stage costume interpretations of classical dress can do this. Therefore, if a designer has absorbed the method of Poussin, he can modify and simplify the antique stage dress of the period to match the mood and method of the drama. Full-bottomed wigs can be replaced by long, wavy hair, heavy overornamentation can be avoided, and complexity in color and texture can be discarded. The structure of the costume can be proportioned and accented to give a formal, rich, artificial, yet classical, look to the play.

Finally, if the designer and director choose a more contemporary mode of production, an abstract, "no-period" approach may be taken, or modified full-dress formal wear may be used to match the formality and classical restraint of Racine. A modern design for the palace background can also have all of the coolness and simplicity of Racine's dramaturgy.

Thus, whatever approach is chosen, the textures in sets and costumes should not be complicated and varied. A single texture may be used as a major unifying element in all costumes, with ornament used only as accent and to give focus to certain areas in the dress. Colors should be selected from the clear, cool, rich hues of Poussin, with each costume limited to a single major color and metallic or neutral accent. The lines of the costumes should be imposing, formal, graceful, and theatrical, with full use of long mantles and trailing gowns (Fig. 60).

But what of the comparable classical visual demands of the comedies of Molière? In many ways these comedies (as distinct from the farces) demand the same sense of symmetry, simplicity, precision, and concentration of focus that the plays of Racine demand, but now the setting is bourgeois, and we do not need the classical or historical material of Poussin for inspiration. A bourgeois classical painter, such as the Dutch artist Vermeer, who presented middle-class interiors of the late seventeenth century in a classical manner, can be of great use as a source for furniture and interior details, and more importantly as a guide for the precise, concentrated, and careful organization of these interior elements into a quiet, perfected, classical simplicity.

Figure 60
Costume designs by the author for a production of
Phèdre by Racine, produced at the University of
Kansas City in 1958. From the collection of the
author

Let us take Molière's *Tartuffe* as an example of a typical French classical comedy. The play is a composite of borrowings from Italian comedy and a strong inheritance both in story line and classical method from the comedies of Terence. Again, the unities of time, place, and action prevail, and the play moves forward in one movement from beginning to end without subplot or excessive use of minor characters. As in most of Molière's plays there is an exaggerated bias or eccentricity in both the protagonist and the antagonist, countered always by a man of reason, such as Cléante, who acts as a commentator on the action and represents Molière's belief in common sense. Tartuffe is the evil catalyst in the action. His character is primarily developed by others until his first appearance at the beginning of the third act; in his two love scenes he is free to develop fully his personality as a repressed sensualist. Orgon is the real protagonist of the piece, a man of foolish good nature whose gullibility allows Tartuffe's plans to mature and flourish. As a prosperous businessman he feels a bit guilty about his money and so gives impulsively and overgenerously to a man he feels is worthier than he. When Tartuffe is exposed, he still cannot distinguish between hypocrisy and piety, and so wants to turn his back on all religion. Unlike Cléante, he cannot take the balanced view.

The humor in the play derives from the psychological responses of characters to unusual situations, and all character deviations from the ideal of common sense established by Cléante (and the maid Dorine) are sharply ridiculed by Molière. The theme of the play is the importance of the balanced life; a secondary theme, which goes back to Roman comedy and the commedia dell'arte, is the folly of a forced marriage.

In his comedies, Molière usually wrote in the rhymed couplet of the French alexandrine, but his thought process was essentially that of realistic prose. His use of verse was clever, witty, and fully able to express idiosyncracies of character, but it was seldom used for idealized poetic purposes. To play the comedies in prose translation, however, is to miss the witty comment made on the traditional alexandrine verse form, and only the polished symmetry and precision of English rhyming couplets can approximate Molière's verse style. The rhythmic flow of his comedies is closely tied to the polished delivery of the verse, and it moves with a sprightly, direct, onward movement from beginning to end, without sharp contrasts, abrupt breaks, or strong shifts of mood. It is this movement that gives Molière's plays their urbaneness and classical, gemlike clarity of mood.

The visual requirements in *Tartuffe* are sharply limited, as they are in most of Molière's plays: a room in Orgon's house with a table, several chairs, a closet, a door, and probably a staircase for Tartuffe's first entrance are all that are required. The play can be produced in any period as long as the costumes and setting are closely related to the personality and social standing of each character and to the simplicity and order of the play's structure. The lighting need not be varied at all, since in Molière's day chandeliers hung over the acting area, giving an appropriate static lighting to the entire play.

In designing a modern production of *Tartuffe* the stress should always be on the simplicity and clarity of the writing, not on a display of the sensuous richness found in the period of the play's composition. In general, a representative selection of recent stage settings for the play falls into two groups: those that stress the structure and balance of the play in a simple, semiabstract way, and those that attempt a realistic bourgeois interior. If the director wants to stress the symmetry and balance of the play's structure and the universality of the characters, then an abstract architectural background is appropriate; if he wants to stress Orgon's bourgeois temperament and taste, then the setting may approach the realistic. In either case the production should not be loaded with decorative accessories. Only those items that will clearly reveal character and the personality of the household should be used. In costume, if a semirealistic mood is wanted then the costumes should have more variety in line, texture, and color; if an abstract architectural background is used, the color and texture of the costumes should be limited, but the shape and structure of the costume should be stressed (see Fig. 2).

One of the best visual sources for designing a production of a Molière play is the work of Vermeer. Both his classical spirit and his bourgeois settings are similar to Molière's; even when *Tartuffe* is produced in a period other than the seventeenth century, Vermeer's subtle and simple use of color, line, and texture can give the designer insight into how to translate the verbal methods of Molière into the visual designs for the play (Fig. 61).

Vermeer used color in a clear, cool way, with subtle shifts of light, and he always achieved great variety through subtle color variations. A designer can make excellent use of this method by restricting his color palette in a similar way and by limiting the number of colors used in a set or a particular costume (see Fig. 3). For costumes, using a basic hue accented or complemented by another color or a neutral color is much more effective than using many hues, values, and intensities. The same is true of texture: one texture for all major costumes, accented with a contrasting texture, will lend both clarity and simplicity to the production. For example, a crisp, subtly shining bengaline faille, with variations in rib and sheen, can be used and then accented with velvet ribbons in various widths and limited amounts. When this simplicity in texture is used, then the line of the costume becomes extremely important, and the silhouette of each costume must be exactly right. The width of a cuff, the flair of a bow, the fall of a length of lace, the size of the curls on a wig—all become very important when the method of design is so spare and intellectually planned. If the individual, satiric character of the costumes and the simple bourgeois or abstract architectural background of the set match the polished acting required by the script, then the performance of *Tartuffe* will be as pleasing visually, despite its simplicity, as it is verbally.

Finally, some comment should be made on the differences between Restoration comedy and the comedies of Molière. The aristocrats who returned to England with King Charles II in 1660 had spent the majority of their exile in France. For all the pride that the court of the new "merry

Figure 61
Vermeer. *A Lady and Gentleman at the Virginals,* ca. 1664. An example of the cool, carefully composed, classical bourgeois interiors. Vermeer was a contemporary of Molière, and his compositional method was quite similar to the French playwright's. Courtesy The Lord Chamberlain, St. James's Palace, London.

monarch" took in its French taste, and for all the borrowings from France in playwriting, clothing, interior decoration, and furniture, there was still an unmistakably British tone to Restoration culture. It lacked the precise organization and neoclassical structure of the French court style of Louis XIV and the excessive grandeur found in the ceremonial court of the Sun King. Which is not to say that the Restoration lacked a sense of great display; a room of the Restoration period appears very aristocratic and grand, until it is compared to a room at Versailles. The formal coldness and rigid structuring of the French room contrasts strongly with the English room, which is a rich and comfortable pastiche of decorative Baroque style (Fig. 62).

In the portraits of the leaders of Restoration society by Peter Lely, there is much more stress on the casual and the sensual than on the formal and the grand (Fig. 63). These portraits, as well as Restoration interiors, can assist the designer in capturing that exact mixture of sparkling brilliance, elegant sensuality, and relaxed yet organized structure that was so distinctive in Restoration comedies.

Restoration comedies are noted for their sharp wit, brilliant dialogue, sophisticated characters, and amoral situations rather than for their clear-cut plots and direct storytelling. Although Restoration comedies derive from the comedies of Molière, they differ from Molière's comedies in the following ways: Molière wrote his comedies with a minimum of characters, no subplots, and within unities of time, place, and action, whereas the Restoration playwrights, in the manner of their Elizabethan predecessors, used more characters, complicated plots with one or two subplots, and changes of setting. Molière's themes were strongly moral, whereas the themes of the majority of the Restoration playwrights had a somewhat amoral bent, where superior (if sometimes cynical) self-knowledge was rewarded and foolishness punished (the plays imply that man is corruptible and his corruptibility must be accepted with a sophisticated, worldly tolerance); Molière stressed the ideal of moderation and balance, the Restoration playwrights stressed self-knowledge.

Figure 62
The Double-Cubed Room at Wilton House near Salisbury, ca. 1649. Designed by John Webb under the influence of Inigo Jones. An example of the more eclectic and less formal classical style that was admired in England during the Restoration. Courtesy the Earl of Pembroke, Salisbury, England

Baroque Theatre

Baroque Theatre

110

Let us look briefly at *The Relapse,* a play written in 1696 by Sir John Vanbrugh, who was a courtier and part-time architect. (He designed the famous Blenheim Palace for the Duke of Marlborough.) The play was written in answer to a play by Colley Cibber called *Love's Last Shift,* because Vanbrugh did not think that Cibber's play presented an accurate picture of human nature. *The Relapse* is based, as is so often the case in comedy, on an exchange of identities, and it has two quite separate plots. One plot follows the fortunes of the newly married Loveless and Amanda; the other follows the fortunes of Fashion and the arranged marriage of his brother, Lord Foppington, to the daughter of a country squire named Sir Tunbelly Clumsy. There are many complications and amours until Loveless is finally seduced by the amorous Berinthia and Lord Foppington loses his intended wife to his brother.

The plot's complications are far less interesting than the characters. Lord Foppington is a particularly outstanding example of the overweening and pretentious fop, whose dressing scene is a high point in the production and a challenge to the designer. Everything about the personality and character of Lord Foppington is exuberantly excessive and overdrawn and he is the perfect butt of all the commentary and satire throughout the play. The other characters are either exaggerated caricatures, such as Sir Tunbelly Clumsy and the matchmaker, Coupler, or worldly sophisticates who know just how to play the aristocratic games of love so admired by Restoration society.

The language is witty and clever, filled with exaggerated expletives and expressions coined by Lord Foppington, and licentious and suggestive repartee from those involved in the game of love. The theme is appropriately involved with the relapse of a supposedly true love and the discomfiture of the man of excess. The rhythm of the play is dictated by the need to structure the two plot lines into intertwining and overlapping scenes; there is thus no through line of development, but a casual balancing of scenes of excess with scenes of wit, and a series of individual rhythms rather than one overall rhythm.

Figure 63
Peter Lely. *Two Ladies of the Lake Family,* ca. 1666. An example of the soft, casual, sensual elegance preferred in English portraiture during the Restoration. Courtesy The Tate Gallery, London

In a Restoration production of *The Relapse* a number of settings were necessary for scenes in town and in the country house of Sir Tunbelly Clumsy. Each would have been a separate room formed with wings and shutters; the occasional pieces of furniture would have been carried on and off by servants. The costumes would have been the rich contemporary fashions of the day except for the laughable exaggerated clothes of Foppington and the country garb of Sir Tunbelly Clumsy and his daughter, Hoydon.

The play could be presented today with a certain quaintness by using the wing and shutter system or, more casually, folding screens. If the presentation of full interiors is desired, then a turntable system may be useful. In all productions, the designer should use Restoration interiors and the structure of the play as a guide, and he will then catch some of the rich imbalances and the casual and subtle asymmetries that make Restoration plays so different from French comedy. Costumes should take their lead from the fashion drawings of the day and the ideals expressed in the paintings of Lely, who stressed elegant sophistication and sensuousness, careful fit and casualness, all at the same time. Rich fabrics with hard surfaces that reflect light should be used (analogous to the sharpness of the wit and the sparkle of the dialogue) (Fig. 64).

Figure 64
A scene from *The Relapse,* produced by the American Conservatory Theatre, 1970. Photo by Hank Kranzler, San Francisco, California

114

5

Eighteenth Century Theatre

The eighteenth century was a period of transition from the Baroque to romanticism. It was a period that saw the last coherent western European style, the Rococo, come to an end and be superseded by bourgeois subjectivism and sentimentality.

The courtly art of the Rococo was an anticlimax, a dying fall of art devoted to monarchical and aristocratic grandeur. A slackening of personal and social discipline, a growing skepticism about religion, a decadence among the nobility, and a great feminine bias in art and culture created by the artistic and social power of the mistresses of Louis XV ushered in an age of refinement, elegance, and sentimental sensibility that is best exemplified in the paintings of Watteau. Despite their joyful surrender to reality and pleasure, Watteau's delicate *fêtes galantes* were full of melancholy and nostalgia—a yearning for the Arcadian ideal of uniting sophisticated sensibility and emotion, the material and the spiritual, the weighty intelligence and the frivolous (Fig. 65). The ornamental and decorative style of the Rococo, like Watteau's shepherds and shepherdesses, seems to drift effortlessly in a delicate and airy landscape. Only in England was such aristocratic day-dreaming inhibited by a commercial aristocracy that reflected bourgeois sentiment and morality.

Figure 65
Watteau. *Les Plaisirs du Bal,* ca. 1719. An example of the aristocratic and artificial dreamworld of the eighteenth century French artist who invented the *fête galante.* Courtesy Governors of Dulwich College Picture Gallery, London

The Rococo gradually declined around the middle of the eighteenth century. The continuous attack of bourgeois taste that led to its decline came from two directions: the sentimentality and naturalism of Jean Jacques Rousseau, Samuel Richardson, and William Hogarth; and the rationalism and classicism of Gotthold Lessing, Johann Winckelmann and Jacques Louis David. Instead of the courtly softness and decadence of the Rococo, both groups emphasized an ideal of simplicity, earnestness, clarity, and morality. The realistic, narrative paintings of Greuze, with their sentimental bourgeois morality, represented the new middle-class artistic taste that tended to read art for its moral story rather than see it as a visual composition (Fig. 66).

The works of David represented a renewal of the taste for the classical and the rational in painting. David's works appealed to a sense of personal honor and civic virtue, and a triumph over aristocratic decadence that harked back to the ideal of Poussin (Fig. 67). Both the picturesque romanticism and the severe classicism that developed side by side in the later part of the eighteenth century represented the concept of association, whereby all art forms were admired not for their intrinsic value but for their ability to evoke rich, emotional associations with life, history, and literature. From the neoclassical temples in the city to the neo-Gothic villas in the country, from the republican virtues in the paintings of David to the romantic ruins in the paintings of Hubert Robert, we can see how such art appealed to middle-class, snobbish ideas about learning, prestige, and position (Fig. 68). By the early years of the nineteenth century the notion of sentimental association as an artistic ideal had spread throughout Europe, and led to the tasteless eclecticism that was to reign in Europe until the opening of the twentieth century.

During the eighteenth century theaters increased in size to accommodate the larger, middle-class audiences, but staging methods in general were similar to those of the Baroque. In theaters on the Continent, where the forestage and proscenium doors were nonexistent, the action took place on a narrow plane to the front of the raked stage in front of

Figure 66
Greuze. *The Return of the Prodigal,* 1781. An example of the moralistic, sentimental painting admired by Denis Diderot in the late eighteenth century. Courtesy The French Musées Nationaux

Figure 67
David. *The Lictors Bringing to Brutus the Bodies of His
Sons,* 1789. An example of the coldness and austerity
in the new classicism of David, who stressed the
stoic virtues and civic duty in classical antiquity.
Courtesy the French Musées Nationaux

Figure 68
Robert. *The Pont du Gard,* ca. 1787. An example of
the romantic ruins that became one of the most
popular subjects in the late eighteenth century.
Courtesy the French Musées Nationaux

scenery whose sight lines vanished either centerstage or symmetrically off to either side of the stage. The grand drape was used only at the opening and closing of the performance, while "transformations" and other scenery changes were made in full view of the audience using the chariot system. Stage wings and shutters were moved on and off stage by the turning of a single winch in the basement. Small chariots or carts on tracks supported the wings and shutters on masts that came up through slits in the stage floor. The best example of this system at work today is in the Royal Theatre of the Palace of Drottningholm in Sweden (Fig. 69). In British theaters, where action took place on a wider fore-stage with many entrances and exits through proscenium doors, a groove system was used for changing scenery; flats were moved on and off stage by means of tracks or grooves set into the stage floor.

As the eighteenth century matured, scenery moved from the conventional gardens, palaces, and woods of the Baroque to more picturesque, individualized, and historically objective settings, and stage lighting moved toward more mood and atmosphere in both the chiaroscuro of the scene paintings and the actual illumination of the stage. More individual set pieces, drops, and cut-out wings were added to give variety to the stage scene, and costumes moved slowly but confidently to historical accuracy, more appropriateness to character, and less conventional effects. In England, Charles Macklin introduced the idea of plaids for Macbeth's costume, David Garrick performed Richard III in approximations of Elizabethan dress, and Sarah Siddons and John Philip Kemble introduced actual classical garments into Shakespeare's classical plays at the end of the century. Even at the Comédie Française, Voltaire, in league with Mlle Clairon and Henri Louis Lekain, brought about many changes that led to greater realism.

Although the eighteenth century was a period of transition, the descriptive words that continually reappear in any assessment of the art and culture of the period, particularly its drama, are "sentimental" and

Figure 69
Stage setting, Royal Theater, Drottningholm, Sweden, ca. 1765. One of the few extant examples of a stage house completely equipped with stage scenery and machinery of the eighteenth century. Courtesy Drottningholms Teatermuseum

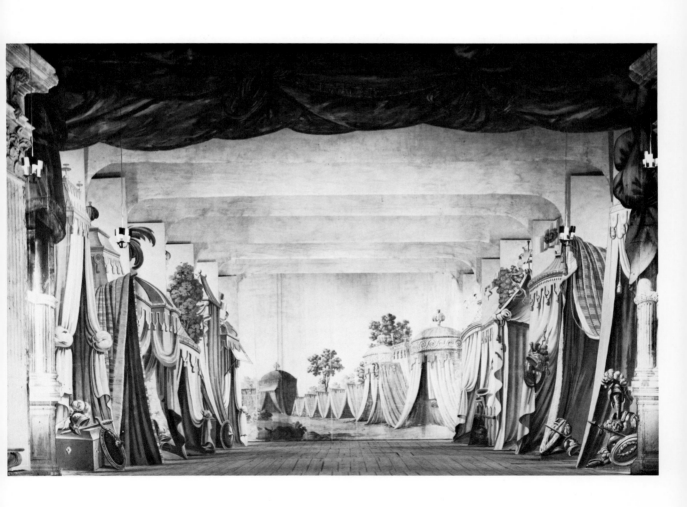

"moralizing." Even the best playwrights of the period, such as Beaumarchais, Goldsmith, Sheridan, and Goldoni, who worked to reestablish a true comedy of laughter, projected a certain sentimentality and moral tone that distinguished their works from those of other comic playwrights. Sheridan's *The School for Scandal,* sometimes said to be the greatest comedy of manners in the English language, was written to escape the excesses of sentimental comedy. There was still a strong note of sentiment and morality in the play, however, and it in no way achieved the worldly wit and amoral tone of Restoration comedy.

Sheridan's structural approach in the play was closer to English Elizabethan comedy than it was to Molière's comedies. He used both a major and a minor plot line, which at first have little connection, but gradually entwine in a common resolution. If one judges *The School for Scandal* by its storytelling, then real praise is in order for the way in which the playwright was able to carry his audience from one scene to another with ease. Sheridan maintained an easy casualness and a sure sense of control throughout fourteen different scenes that took place in four different households. The tour de force of the play has always been the famous "screen scene," where all the preceding conflicts in the action were brought together and exposed through a series of comic reversals that finally revealed Lady Teazle behind the screen. Then, like the final pieces in a puzzle, all the loose ends are tied together and the play has the expected happy conclusion.

Sheridan developed fully and clearly the personalities of Joseph, Charles, Sir Peter, and Lady Teazle, and deftly characterized the members of the school for scandal through their names and a mere attribute or two. The scandalmongers in the play set the tone of the action and are used for exposition and for initiating conflict. In many ways they give unity and point to the play, and are often the freshest and most humorous part of modern productions. Although their viciousness is too superficial to be a real threat to the leading characters, they are always available to complicate or untangle the plot and set the desired comic tone for the play. Whenever there was a sense of ambiguity about thoughts or motives, the characters were allowed to make direct asides to the audience.

The themes of both *The School for Scandal* and Molière's *Tartuffe* relate to the unmasking of hypocrisy, but in *Tartuffe* religious hypocrisy is a real threat to the individual and society, whereas in *The School for Scandal* the social hypocrisy of Joseph Surface and the scandalmongers is never a serious threat. Sheridan's play reflects the lighter touch of the eighteenth century; it is more a defense of the new "natural man" than an attack on the aristocratic social order. At the same time that the play attacks false sentiment and morality, it finally illustrates the standard lesson in all eighteenth century sentimental literature—that virtue will be rewarded and evil punished.

The language of the play gives the play its tone of polished wit; the characters generally make their points with elegant epigrams and witty descriptions that make each conversation appear sparkling, spontaneous, and clever. Far removed from the language of everyday life, such conversational brilliance reflects that sophisticated group in upper-class English society, which, although wealthy and admired, was also artificial and rather useless. The sharp, rapid, witty dialogue and the polished movement and speech of the actors, rather than the vagaries of plot complication, establish the light and easy rhythm of the play.

The play reflects very specifically the social scene in London in 1777, and we are fortunate in having an engraving of a performance at Drury Lane in 1788 that is probably an accurate representation of the original sets and costumes (Fig. 70). It is important for a contemporary designer to note that the actors' costumes closely approximated those worn by members of the audience, the wings and shutters were arranged in a way that suggested a three-walled interior, and the stage had a wide apron and proscenium doors. Many set pieces and properties were painted into the set and not actually used.

In presenting *The School for Scandal* for a contemporary audience the

Figure 70
"The Screen Scene" from *The School for Scandal* by
Sheridan, produced at Drury Lane Theatre, London,
1778. An example of the forestage, proscenium
doors, stage boxes, wings, shutters, and contemporary dress found in an English production of the
late eighteenth century. From an engraving of the
period. Courtesy Victoria and Albert Museum,
Crown Copyright

Figure 71
"The School" in *The School for Scandal,* produced
at the Queen's Theatre, London, 1937. An example
of elegant but exaggerated fashions for satirical
effect. Photo by Houston Rogers, London

director must decide whether to echo the visual methods of the original production or to use one of a number of possible contemporary approaches. A certain sophisticated period charm often can be achieved by combining the use of wings and shutters changed in full view of the audience by servants in livery, although the painting of these wings and shutters may reflect a contemporary artistic approach to the decorative aspects of architectural ornamentation.

There are other approaches, of course. The scenes could be designed as realistic, period box sets, for example, or the play could be done in the round with carefully chosen period furniture, on a thrust stage with only a suggestion of eighteenth century decor backing the action, on an open stage with a few architectural, decorative, set pieces to set the tone of the play, or within a permanent eighteenth century architectural framework with only furniture shifted from scene to scene. In all these approaches, the stress should be on capturing the casual elegance and light informality of the eighteenth century English social world that is the basis for the entire play (Fig. 71).

There are roughly two ways in which a designer might approach the problem of costume design for the play: one, a detailed, psychologically based, character approach; the other, a more limited, abstract, decorative approach, in which individual designs are less important than an overall effect of mood and period style. Whatever the approach, the casualness, elegance, and artificiality of eighteenth century culture should be clearly evident. Fabrics for the most part should be crisp, shiny, and brittle with soft accents, such as lace. Color should be light and gay with a few dark accents on the trim. Characters belonging to a low social order should be clothed in dark garments. The line and shape of the costumes should reflect both the soft, sentimental lines of the clothing worn by younger women of the period and the more formal lines worn by the powerful leaders of the period. A designer should refer particularly to the paintings of Gainsborough, where one finds the soft lines and fabrics, reflective of a sentimental, semiromantic ideal, side by side with hard lines and fabrics, reflective of a more brittle, formal, and artificial society (Fig. 72). By examining the styles of the period, a designer will learn how to create humor in certain costumes by means of minimal exaggeration. For example, Lady Teazle's naïve attempts to fit into society and the crass and heavy personality of a Lady Sneerwell or a Mrs. Candour can be beautifully illuminated by slight exaggerations of costume line.

Figure 72
Gainsborough. *Mrs. Graham,* ca. 1785. An example
of the delicacy, elegance, and light brushwork of
this Rococo portrait painter. Courtesy The National
Gallery of Scotland

Romantic Theatre

128

6

Romantic Theatre

Romanticism as a fully conscious western European style was impossible until the late eighteenth century, because European society since the Renaissance had been based on a caste system that placed great emphasis on form and organization in both society and the arts. Not until the French Revolution did artists forcefully break from the strictures and inhibitions of the aristocratic-bourgeois world to the lonely, alienated, existential world of emotion and subjectivity. The leaders of romanticism, in their drive to break with the assumed mediocrity of the present, tried to escape into a world that was more exciting, more fulfilling, more beautiful, and more terrifying than the bourgeois, industrial world developing at the opening of the nineteenth century. What romanticists lacked was a technique for expressing their personal and subjective reactions to life. Delacroix, for example, one of the great romantic painters, had to turn to Rubens for his artistic method, and throughout his long career he never achieved a technique with enough power to express his exciting, theatrical emotions (Fig. 73). The British painter Turner came close to a new method with his "hot scrubbed pigment" and

Figure 73
Delacroix. *Dante and Virgil in Hell,* 1822. An example of the exotic subject matter, violent movement, rich color, and loose, thick brush stroke used in the romantic paintings of Delacroix. Courtesy the French Musées Nationaux

Romantic Theatre

130

"tinted steam" (Fig. 74). It remained for Van Gogh and the expressionists, however, to find an artistic method that could express their subjective feelings. The Baroque, Renaissance, and medieval borrowings of the romanticists showed both a search for method and an escape to the past.

The romanticists' psychotic fear of the present and deep desire to find a haven, an answer, or a release into a new world of the imagination often led to a kind of pompous exaggerated eclecticism in their art and a new view of history. Previously, history had been viewed as an unfolding and continual drama of progress toward a known goal, but now the future became a fearful unknown, the processes of society and government became immutable. At the same time that western man became more aware of the past, he became more alienated from the historical continuum of western civilization than he had been in any previous period. Romanticism, rooted in the torment of the individual mind and the feeling of homelessness brought on by this new concept of man in history, was the first awakening of modern anxiety, existentialism, and relativism in art, science, and morality. Romantic art was the first complete and conscious human document, in which the tormented personal confession was acceptable as a legitimate subject in art and literature.

Romanticism also nurtured the complete alienation of the artist from society; art became autonomous, a creation by artists for artists. Romantic artists and writers saw themselves as part of a new aristocracy that had risen above the rest of society—as half-seers, half-bohemians, removed from the moral and cultural values of their fellow men. With their introspection and self-analysis, they saw themselves as strangers, as fascinating but fearful unknowns, and replaced experience in the world with self-experience and natural objects with an unbounded interest in a "second self."

Theaters of the early nineteenth century were generally exceedingly large (Fig. 75). The great repertory companies on the Continent, such as the Comédie Française and the Vienna Burgtheater, were government

Figure 74
Turner. *Rain, Steam and Speed,* 1844. An example
of Turner's tempestuous, "scrubbed-in" brush work,
by which he hoped to express the cosmic power
behind the elements of air, fire, and water. Courtesy
National Gallery, London

Romantic Theatre

132

supported, while in England the theaters with a royal patent, such as Covent Garden and Drury Lane, had to rely on the box-office attraction of their acting talent. With the advent of the railroads, the older repertory system was replaced by the concept of the "long run" and the tour, where a production was used as a vehicle for a star performer. The rise of the star system and the long run gradually changed theatre in the later nineteenth century into a money-making business investment rather than an art form. The kinds of performances ranged from variety entertainment and circuses to grand opera and the classics. In fact, the theatre became a mass entertainment media, much like television is today, to accommodate the new audience, which changed from an eighteenth century, middle-class minority to a truly mass audience, especially with the influx of lower-class people who flooded the industrialized cities looking for work. Theaters now frequently seated as many as 3,000 spectators in the larger cities. The seats on the sloped lower floor were relatively expensive, the boxes contained the most exclusive seats, and the one, two, and sometimes even three balconies contained the moderate and inexpensive seats. Performances, which lasted from seven o'clock until after midnight, often included a play, short acts of singing and dancing, a short comedy, and even a one-act light opera.

Staging methods during the nineteenth century were dominated by an ever-increasing drive for historical accuracy in settings and costumes, and the stage became more and more cluttered with attempts to suggest a detailed reality about past times and faraway places, even when the aim of the romantic dramatists was to escape into an idealized past. In the works of romantic playwrights like Hugo and Byron, the importance of individual detail or character set in a particular time and place replaced the more generalized, contemporary, and even cavalier cultural outlook of the past. Plays were written that demanded many historical settings and scenes of high pageantry; even Shakespearean revivals became an excuse to present to the public a great museum of historical facts and effects. This method reached its zenith in the early 1850s with

Figure 75
The interior of the Drury Lane Theatre by Pugin
and Rowlandson, 1808. From Ackermann's *Microcosm
of London,* 1808. An example of the enormous size
of an English theatre in the early nineteenth century.
Courtesy The Metropolitan Museum of Art, Harris
Brisbane Dick Fund, 1917

the Shakespearean revivals of Charles Kean, which required months of preparation by the teams of art historians and archaeologists who were gathering background material for the production. The program notes were very extensive for these productions, which were intended to teach and enlighten rather than emotionally involve the spectator (Fig. 76).

The scenery for such productions was still primarily painted in perspective upon a back-cloth (rather than shutters) framed by a series of perspective wings that were frequently quite solid and three dimensional. The wings were sometimes moved on and off stage by grooves in the stage floor or on chariots whose masts came up through floor slits from the basement, but many larger pieces were moved on and off stage manually. Wings and set pieces were arranged asymmetrically to create an illusion of reality, an illusion further aided by the use of framing pieces and perspective backdrop, and the adoption of gas lighting, which allowed for the dimming and raising of light on the stage and the possibility of far more theatrical effects than in the past. Throughout this period the stage floor remained raked for perspective effect; only with experiments in the 1840s in three-walled "box" sets for plays set in contemporary interiors did the theatre gradually shift to flat acting areas.

Costumes were based on accuracy, not on art; unity, beauty, and theatricality were much less admired than authenticity of detail. What resulted was a piling up of complex detail with little regard for the overall artistic effect. Mrs. Kean, for example, in *The Winter's Tale,* added a Victorian crinoline and hairdo to a very authentic Greek costume, without anyone questioning the final result (Fig. 77). The gain during this period was obviously in planning and research, not in artistry.

There were many great plays of historical pageantry written during this period that were vehicles for star actors and an excuse for heavy production, but few of them have retained both a literary and a theatrical reputation down to the present day. Goethe's *Faust,* although more literary than theatrical in its size, breadth of action, and method of development, has managed to keep its place as one of the greatest romantic

Figure 76
Charles Kean as Richard II in a production of Shakespeare's *Richard II* at the Princess Theatre, London, 1857, directed and produced by Charles Kean. An example of the ideal if not the fact of archaeological realism in historical dress. Photo from Clement Scott's *The Drama of Yesterday and Today,* vol. 1

Figure 77
Mrs. Charles Kean as Hermione in a production of
A Winter's Tale at the Princess Theatre, London,
1856. An example of the ambiguities in costume
effect achieved by an actress who continued to wear
Victorian petticoats under a Greek chiton. An engraving from Joseph Jefferson's *Autobiography*

Figure 78
Mr. George Alexander as Faust in the Henry Irving
production of Goethe's *Faust* at the Lyceum Theatre,
London, 1887. The costume is an excellent example
of the detailed yet sharply modified period realism
used in nineteenth century romantic productions.
From Gebbie and Gebbie, *The Stage and Its Stars*,
vol. 2. Courtesy Norman Philbrick Library

dramas and one of the most frequently produced plays of the period, despite its heavy demands. The play is a summation of Goethe's ideals and his growth as a writer (part 1 was begun in 1780 and part 2 was not published until 1831). It was the very personal record of Goethe's quest for the meaning of life that made *Faust* such an important romantic theatre epic (Fig. 78).

Like most romantic dramas that present a sweepingly vast picture of life, *Faust* has a diffuse and loosely connected plot structure. Although obviously modeled on Shakespeare's large-scaled dramas, it has none

of the economy of effect or unity of action found in *Othello* or *Macbeth*. While Shakespeare, in his mature dramas, invariably set his basic dramatic situation at the beginning of the play, Goethe waited until the fourth scene of *Faust* to pick up the dramatic action through the pact made between Faust and Mephistopheles. Thus, the introductory material of the two prologues took up a great deal of time, aspects of Faust's search were extended or contracted at will, and the amount of attention focused on each character was determined by Goethe's personal preference, not by the action. In short, Goethe was theatrically and romantically self-indulgent. Only in a full, two-evening presentation can the entire story be told, and in many ways part 1 is merely a prologue to part 2.

Even when part 1 is produced alone, the action is spread over two prologues, twenty-five scenes, and sixteen changes of locale. Time and place shift rapidly, many very complicated scenic effects are required, and the costumes and masks for the Walpurgis Night scene are a most difficult challenge for the designer.

Only a minimal number of characters in the large cast are developed with any psychological reality. Faust, Mephistopheles, Wagner, Gretchen, Martha, Valentine, and Lieschen have some three-dimensionality of character, but the rest of the cast are mere abstractions designated by group labels. As in all romantic literature and drama, characterization was concentrated in the emotions and psychology of the hero, Faust. Only as the other characters illustrated, gave insight into, and illuminated Faust's mind and personality was Goethe interested in them.

The theme of *Faust* is established in the first prologue: though man cannot avoid loneliness, suffering, and grievous mistakes of judgment, he can achieve salvation through striving for a better world. Parts 1 and 2 of the drama are a large-scaled dramatization of this optimistic view of man's innate strength and capability in struggling for the betterment of his fellow man. In presenting the ageless problem of good versus evil, Goethe used the imagery of darkness and light in a very romantic way. Faust's carnal, selfish, and narrow love for Gretchen ends in the darkness of Gretchen's death. In part 2, even when Faust thinks he has achieved the light in his love for Helen, his love turns out to be fleeting and transitory. True enlightenment comes only through service to man.

The language of this romantic drama is infinitely varied and complex with many moments when the total effect of rich poetic imagery and soaring rhythms is very impressive. Some of the long poetic speeches are like arias in an opera, used to build the great philosophic themes of the drama without in any way furthering the action. The general rhythmic pattern consists of great sweeping crescendos and abrupt shifts and contrasts, as the dialogue travels from scenes of interior monologue to scenes of exterior action and pageantry. The use of the spoken word, song, dance, folk festival, supernatural voices, and dramatized visions gives an endless series of effects that assault the senses and give great variety to the rhythmic progression of the play. At no point in the drama could the rhythm be said to be light-hearted and gay; it remains heavy, sonorous, symphonic, and grand throughout.

The staging requirements for the two parts of *Faust* are very demanding. Because the play was originally conceived for the stage of the imagination, the challenge to choreographer, costumer, set designer, musicians, lighting designer, and stage director is immense. To orchestrate all the visual effects of the action is a stupendous task that involves calling into play every possible effect upon the senses and imagination of the audience and challenges the total resources of the theatre. Certainly an epic cosmic drama like *Faust* should not be produced today as a historic recreation of how the play might have been produced by Goethe at Weimar. Instead, the structure, theme, poetic imagery, and rhythm of this sweeping, romantic drama must be kept clearly in mind.

One direct and quite frequent approach to the production of *Faust* is to use the image of light and darkness from the play as the organizing factor in the drama, and to present only small set pieces rising out of darkness and symbolizing a world that cannot be seen. Shafts of light are used to suggest the cosmic nature of the action and are theatrically effective in concentrating attention upon a single figure or a small group or in expanding focus into the larger illumination of a full stage scene.

Another more modern approach would be to admit, as does Pirandello in *Six Characters in Search of an Author,* that the stage is just a stage and the characters merely actors "describing" or "presenting" an action. Because of its prologue in heaven, *Faust* lends itself to this interpretation, where everything beyond the prologue becomes a cosmic charade of the meaning of salvation. The stage, with the realities of this world suggested by a few stage properties, and changes of locale indicated by the lighting or projections, thus becomes a cosmic platform for events. The costumes would have a certain reality, but even they would be "costumes," not character clothes.

Probably the most popular approach in contemporary German theatre is a production that applies ultramodern concepts in art to full sets and costumes to overwhelm the senses of the audience. One line of attack is to use heavy organic textures, rich color, and broken lines to capture the emotional, romantic, subjective, sensuous grandeur of the play. In a 1967 production of part 1 of *Faust* at the Vienna Burgtheater, Faust's study contained a desk constructed of scraps of broken iron, pieces of wood, and small pieces of leather and paper set against a wall that was a collage of wood framing, broken books, bits of leather, pieces of manuscript, and ends of old painted cloth, all sprayed and aged to the color and texture of the interior of an old cave. The production was a total assault on the senses and beautifully symbolized the dusty decay in Faust's mind in a completely modern way. This approach did lack, however, a strong underlining of the intellectual, philosophical content of the drama.

In a 1966 production of part 2 of *Faust* at the Schiller Theater in Berlin an almost opposite approach was taken. An abstract, geometric approach was used, which stressed the intellectual aspects of the play. The settings were composed of glowing, colorless shapes made of plastic or metal, the music was abstract, cosmic, and mysterious, and Helen appeared inside a transparent plastic sphere. The general impression was one of a cosmic no-man's-land between heaven and earth (Fig. 79).

Figure 79
A scene from *Faust,* Part 2, produced by the Schiller Theater of West Berlin in 1966 under the direction of Ernst Schröder. Scenery by Bernhard Heiliger. Costumes by Alexander Comaro. An example of this metaphysical drama produced in terms of extremely contemporary visual images. Courtesy Schiller Theater of West Berlin. Photo by Ilse Buhs

In costume, if the play is done in a symbolic vein, with great stress on shafts of light penetrating into the general stage darkness, heavy, textured materials should be used to produce monumental silhouettes. Large pleats and folds, fur, and one or two large ornaments can add to the monumentality of the figures. A pictorial equivalent for some of these effects may be found in Delacroix's water color of *Faust in his Study* (Fig. 80). In a production where the stage is simply a platform for presentation, the costumes would be accessories applied over the clothing of the actors, and the one rich, full, romantic accent in an otherwise bare production. Such costumes would have the aura of theatrical stage items, even when fully designed to project character and the sweeping, sensuous images of the play. Finally, in a production where the costumes made use of the lines, textures, and colors of modern art, there would be little stress on period. Instead, many layers of texture, such as shredded rope, melted plastics, and burned fabrics, might be used to create silhouettes based on modern sculpture or painting. In a more abstract, geometric production, costumes could be made of smooth surfaces in glazed, metallic, or plastic textures with hard crisp edges.

Figure 80
Delacroix. *Faust in His Study*, 1827. A watercolor
sketch created by this romantic painter after reading
Goethe's great work. Courtesy Fogg Art Museum,
Harvard University. Bequest of Grenville L. Winthrop

7

Realistic Theatre

About the middle of the nineteenth century the idealistic, subjective views of romanticism began to seem meaningless and overblown. Although several revolutions against repressive political regimes had occurred, there was no real reform. The principles of liberty, equality, and fraternity, in the face of the exploitations of the Industrial Revolution, appeared outworn and passé. In a factory system that drew more and more workers into urban slums, the romantic tendency to see solutions to the world's problems in the inner heart, soul, and imagination of man seemed vague and impractical. Intellectual leaders and artists began to insist that dreams and the imagination be put aside in favor of systematic research into human personality and human society. Observation, clinical analysis, and scientific study of people and institutions were to replace the subjective idealism of romanticism.

A major contribution to this new outlook was the positivist philosophy of Auguste Comte, the father of sociology, whose writings between 1830 and the early 1850s argued for the study of society in a carefully controlled, scientific manner. He felt that by using the scientific method, events in society could be predicted and determined in a clear cause-

and-effect relationship. This concept was further reinforced by the published theories of Charles Darwin, who developed the doctrine that all forms of life had developed from a common ancestry, and that evolution was based on the concept of the survival of the fittest. These theories, coupled with those of positivism, suddenly made heredity and environment very important to both sociologist and artist. Behavior became something beyond the control of the individual; only improvements in the external world could better the human condition.

Thus knowledge and truth in the realistic movement were limited to scientific observation; intuition, imagination, visions, and all forms of the supernatural were removed from art and literature. The objective visual reporting made possible by the invention of the camera became a tremendous influence on all the arts during the later half of the nineteenth century. A peephole glance at life, a scene caught by the camera in the corner of a room, on a street corner, or in a cafe, where people and objects were framed by the edge of the film, became a way of seeing for painters and writers alike. The paintings of both Degas and Eakins are excellent examples of how the seemingly accidental views of life became the framework for the carefully planned structural effects and craftsmanship found in realistic plays (Fig. 81).

The very narrowness of the envelope within which a story could be developed led to a great stress on subtlety, form, and intricate character-story relationships. At a time when those opposed to realism were decrying the loss of style in art, the realistic method was leading novelists like Flaubert and playwrights like Ibsen to a new and deeper sense of style—a harsh and demanding craftsmanship and a distilled human poetry which eventually led to symbolism and the abstractions of modern art and literature. Forced to discard the high-flown clichés of romanticism, the realists narrowed their work and vision to go beyond outer action to a study of what Francis Fergusson called the "movement of the psyche." At its peak moments realism triumphed over its limitations of place, character, and language.

Figure 81
Eakins. *The Pathetic Song,* 1881. A brilliant example of the subtle psychological and physical realism of this American artist. Photo courtesy of The Corcoran Gallery of Art, Washington, D.C.

Figure 82
Meissonier. *1814,* 1864. An example of the contrived
academic exercise in painting that was admired for
its technical detail in the salon exhibitions of the
nineteenth century. Courtesy the French Musées
Nationaux

Figure 83
Courbet. *The Funeral at Ornans,* 1849. An example
of the new realism in subject matter and painterly
detail led by the artist Courbet. Courtesy the French
Musées Nationaux

The same was true in painting; realistic artists, such as Courbet, continually rose above the limitations they set for themselves and produced subjective, sensuous responses rather than the cold, scientific responses of salon art, the "academic machine" of the later half of the nineteenth century. For example, Meissonier's *1814 (Napoleon's Retreat from Moscow)* was planned with such attention to scientific detail that the stage setting erected in the artist's studio show took weeks to perfect before it was ready to be painted on canvas (Fig. 82). Its forms were more accurate, more technical, more objectively rendered than the forms in Courbet's *The Funeral at Ornans,* yet the latter transcended scientific reporting and delved deeply into subjectively experienced personal values. In giving up the broad sweep of vision available to artists since the Renaissance for the narrow confines of the everyday scene, the realists either succeeded with sharply focused concentration and depth or failed with a superficial reproduction of certain small areas of life (Fig. 83).

In the theatre of the later part of the nineteenth century, there was a greater attempt than in the past to stage plays with historical reality. More pieces of scenery built in solid three dimensions and more painted perspective backdrops, masked and lit to give as great an illusion of reality as possible, were used. For plays whose action required one or more interiors, movement was entirely away from side set pieces and painted backdrops to the three solid walls and ceiling of a box set. The plays that represented the "new drama" in the middle of the nineteenth century were basically romantic melodramas written under the guise of realism; it wasn't until the plays of Ibsen, Zola, Brieux, and others that the setting and the total visual environment of the action became an integral part of the drama.

Along with an increasing demand for the integration of background and action came the demand for the integration of all other aspects of a production, and thus a need for a stage director. George II, Duke of Saxe-Meiningen, is usually credited with developing the completely integrated, large-scale, realistic production. He himself designed all the scenery and costumes, worked out blocking, picturization, and movement, and organized the extended rehearsal period. With his entire company independent of "stars" and subordinated to the overall stage effect, the "Theatre Duke" spread the gospel of the realistic, ensemble performance for the stage classics of the day in his many tours to the leading cities of Europe (Fig. 84).

It remained for independent, noncommercial groups in Paris, Berlin, and Moscow to introduce staging methods that stressed ensemble acting, realistic settings, and great attention to detail into productions of the new drama of realism. At the Théâtre Libre, founded in Paris in 1887, André Antoine stressed absolute naturalness in his stage pictures, with every property and item of set decoration taken from real life. In the late 1800s and early 1900s, the Freie Bühne in Berlin, the Independent Theatre in London, and the Abbey Theatre in Dublin focused on the new realism, but the group with the most lasting influence, especially

Figure 84
An engraving of the Saxe-Meiningen Court Company in a performance of Shakespeare's *Julius Caesar.* An example of the dynamic and precise planning of crowd scenes that made the work of this company admired throughout Europe. Courtesy Victoria and Albert Museum, Crown Copyright

Realistic Theatre

THE ILLUSTRATED LONDON NEWS.

REGISTERED AT THE GENERAL POST-OFFICE FOR TRANSMISSION ABROAD.

No. 2194.—VOL. LXXVIII.   SATURDAY, JUNE 4, 1881.   TWO WHOLE SHEETS | SIXPENCE. By Post, 6½d.

SCENE FROM "JULIUS CÆSAR," AS PERFORMED AT DRURY LANE THEATRE BY THE SAXE-MEININGEN COURT COMPANY.—SEE PAGE 542.

in the training of actors, was the Moscow Art Theatre, founded in 1898 by Constantin Stanislavsky and Nemirovich-Danchenko (Fig. 85).

Stanislavsky eventually published his theories on actor training in two books, *My Life in Art* and *An Actor Prepares*, and his basic precepts might be summed up as follows: The actor must be superbly developed in the use of body and voice, and in psychological techniques that permit emotional recall of personal experiences that could be related to a particular role. The actor must be able to define and outline the core of his role, particularly the key desires that motivated his character throughout a play, but such knowledge could not be projected to an audience unless the actor could fuse, through concentration, all his onstage work into a single purpose. His response to other actors, his sense of the rhythmic development of the play, and his ability to work continuously toward refinement and perfection in his art were all tied to the ideal of onstage concentration of focus and depth of penetration.

Of the many contributors to the drama of realism the two greatest were undoubtedly Ibsen and Chekov. The former used the careful plotting of the "well-made plays" of Scribe and Sardou, which were in many respects analogous to contemporary mystery melodramas, to project themes of social import. The latter developed the play of mood to project the hidden longings and frustrations of human nature. Ibsen stressed the structure and craftsmanship of his playwriting, while Chekov was so skillful at concealing the mechanics of his work that his audience had the feeling it was seeing scenes from actual life.

Ibsen's *Ghosts*, which depicts the hollowness of a conventional, nineteenth century marriage, is a typical thesis play that also includes the thrills and tricks of Parisian boulevard theater melodrama. On the one hand, the play pretends to be life itself, not art; on the other hand, it is more artfully crafted than any acknowledged "well-made play." The play can be viewed on two structural levels: as a rational welding together of a series of events with a clear-cut moral, and as the "soul" or inner story of the outward action. It is actually organized as a series of debates on conventional morality between Pastor Manders and Mrs.

Figure 85
Act 1 of the original production of Chekov's *The Cherry Orchard* at the Moscow Art Theatre in 1904. An example of the untheatrical, everyday realism practiced by Stanislavsky and his associates in their productions of Chekov's plays. Courtesy Stanford University Drama Department

Alving, Pastor Manders and Oswald, and Oswald and Mrs. Alving. There is a mounting, carefully controlled element of suspense maintained throughout, and each act ends with an exciting moment which sets the issues to date and promises intriguing new developments. But behind the surface events of the story there is the vaguely suggested tragedy of a deep and brooding view of the human condition (Fig. 86).

Each principal character in the play suffers, searches for answers, and gains new personal insights with each new reversal of the action. Mrs. Alving is involved in a search for her true human condition, but as in Sophocles' *Oedipus Rex,* we are shown only the end of the search, when the events of the past are illuminated by the present. Like Oedipus, as one veil after another is removed from the past and the present, Mrs. Alving begins to realize what the past and its dead ideas have done to her. The theme of the play—the "ghosts" of the past that have come to haunt the present—follows her to the end of the drama, and she becomes both a symbol and a very real, warm, and deeply understanding human being. Oswald is both a symbol of dissolution and decline and a very pathetic individual, and Pastor Manders, a mere shell of a man, represents all the clichés about bourgeois morality. Thus all of the major characters are symbols, believable human beings, and stereotypes who might appear in a boulevard melodrama.

Through the fumbling phrases of everyday speech and symbolic words and expressions like the term *ghosts,* Ibsen attempted to lift the dialogue to a hidden poetry of feelings and ideas. There is no verbal music in the play, only this hidden poetry, masquerading as reporting, a poetry of the theatre that can only come alive in an outstanding theatrical performance. There are two levels of rhythm in the play: the rhythm of the everyday life and events within the circumscribed setting of the bourgeois household, and the rhythm that develops the mood, inner suffering, and growing knowledge of the characters. *Ghosts* is a very complex interpenetration of the rhythms of the "well-made play" and the tragic rhythm of the lives of Oswald, Pastor Manders, and Mrs. Alving.

Ibsen's realistic technique can be fully seen in the visual requirements

Figure 86
A scene from Ibsen's *Ghosts,* produced by the National Theatre of Oslo, Norway, 1966. The production approach is that of selective realism. Courtesy National Theatre, Oslo

of the play. The author gives a very detailed and photographically accurate description of a Victorian parlor backed by a large window showing the snowy peaks and exhilarating wilderness beyond the cramped interior. The characters are obviously heavily influenced by their physical environment, and the set and costume designers must treat action and characters with subtlety and awareness, if they are to create an appropriate environment. The movement and action of the play must be based partly on observations from life and partly on a sensitivity to the organizational effects in the structure of the story. Furniture, especially, can be used to assist, block, or complicate the action, and it can be visually arranged to give great meaning to the personal relationships in the play.

In a contemporary production of *Ghosts,* there are not many choices of staging from which the designer can choose. A direct use of stage realism demands a fourth-wall production approach, in which the audience is shown the interior of a room with realistic furnishings and accessories. Therefore, the designer must work with great subtlety and care, because mood, shape, texture, line, and color must all be subordinate to the environmental reality of the stage scene. The single interior demanded in *Ghosts* must give an impression of the intimacy of Mrs. Alving's parlor as well as focus the attention of the audience on the concentrated nature of the play's construction. Each of the five characters must be related to the setting in a way that will illuminate character and the events that have previously transpired in that room. The single most important mood to establish is that of the ghost of Captain Alving—a sense of what the past twenty years of Mrs. Alving's life with this man have been like. Decorative detail should not clutter the walls and furnishings of the set and obscure the primary effects of the mood. A selective realism must be used that balances the fussy disorder of Victorian detail with a careful arrangement of space and furnishings to support character and action (Fig. 87).

Figure 87
Clifford Rose as Engstrand and Natasha Pyne as Regina in Ibsen's *Ghosts,* produced by the Royal Shakespeare Company at the Aldwych Theatre, London, 1967. Designs by Jocelyn Herbert. The costumes show a strong emphasis on textural variety within the confines of realism. Courtesy the Royal Shakespeare Company. Photo by Reg Wilson

Realistic Theatre

Couches, tables, and chairs are the key accessories in the conflicts and debates that take place in Mrs. Alving's parlor, and they must be of an appropriate size and shape to complement and support the stage action. They can act as supports and barriers, as objects to be caressed and pushed around, or as symbols of persons and objects loved and hated. Furniture, more than anything else, can make the blocking pattern most effective in its evocation of a prisonlike atmosphere that has been the center of Mrs. Alving's life since her marriage to Captain Alving. Degas' famous painting of the *Bellelli Family* is an excellent example of how character placement in relation to furniture can reveal personal relationships (Fig. 88): The father faces upstage and is separated from his family by the edge of the fireplace and his chair. The mother dominates one daughter by pulling the girl against her, while the other daughter shows a more independent nature, balanced between the mother and the father. Degas, in his painting entitled *Interior,* or *The Seduction,* also used character placement within a particular furniture arrangement to achieve a heavy and ominous atmosphere (Fig. 89). The woman is seated, weeping at her dressing table, an iron bed illuminated by a small lamp is in the center of the painting on a diagonal, and the man is lost in shadows as he leans on the door at the right. One immediately senses that the man is a threat to the girl, from whom he is separated by two important symbolic objects: the bed at an angle upstage center and an open pistol case on the lamp table. The painting, with its camera-angled "snapshot" effect so dear to realistic painters and set designers, is like the climactic scene from a realistic play.

The costume designs for *Ghosts* must reflect a balance between realistic period clothing for character and a subtle evocation of the mood and atmosphere of the play. The period Norwegian costume sources of 1879 should be both exaggerated and simplified. The thick, heavy, oppressive textures of Victorian dress and the muddied, grayed colors of that era are right for this play. The lines of the costumes should closely follow the period sources but with some slight exaggerations to underline character. Complicated Victorian detail should be put aside in favor of clarity

Figure 88
Degas, *The Bellelli Family,* 1859. An example of family relationships presented by careful placement of members of the family in relation to one another, the furniture, and the room. Courtesy the French Musées Nationaux

of accent and focus that will illuminate character and action in the same way that Ibsen handled details in plotting.

If the range of realism in the theatre is to be understood fully, then it is important to contrast Ibsen's *Ghosts* with Chekov's *The Cherry Orchard.* An appreciation of the differences between the methods of the two playwrights can be very illuminating for the designer, who will want to use their individual approaches to plot and character as the basis for the visual design of their plays.

By the time Chekov wrote *The Cherry Orchard,* the ambitious mechanism of embedding a certain amount of thrilling action into a drama that carried a social thesis or message had begun to fade and the human spirit and human emotions were being presented not in action, but in the pauses of life. *The Cherry Orchard,* devoid of the mechanical plotting of the "well-made play," was constructed around a series of apparently casual incidents—a theatrical poem dealing with the pathos and suffering that accompany individual and social change. The play does not have a theme in the true sense of that word. In the final analysis, *The Cherry Orchard* appeals to the poetic and emotional sensibilities; any so-called theme must be read into the play or interpreted into it in production. Chekov believed that the perceptions that precede rational analysis are the most true in life, so he selected those moments in life when his characters were most vulnerable and open, when their personal situations were most directly felt and perceived. The action of *The Cherry Orchard* is built around four ceremonial family moments that make up the four acts of the play: the arrival from Paris to take up the old way of life again; the pause at sunset when all of the characters fleetingly see themselves and their lives for what they really are; the slightly hysterical party when the announcement about the sale of the cherry orchard is finally made, and the final departure.

In characterization there is a great difference between what we learn about the characters from their conversations and the dimly perceived personal perceptions we gain from watching their actions and silences. Chekov was extremely dependent on the subtle interpretive abilities of

Figure 89
Degas. *Interior: The Rape,* 1874. An example of the seemingly casual peephole view of Parisian life. The placement of furniture and actors, and the use of light are very carefully planned for dramatic effect. Courtesy the H. P. McIlhenny Collection, Philadelphia

his actors, and only in a superbly orchestrated production will the poetic subtleties of his characterizations crystallize. For example, Lopakhin is a man of action and, in a play with a strong social message, could have been used as a symbol of Russia's move into the future, but he is shown at moments of reflection when he is forced to examine his own motives in a rather pathetic way, and we see him in all his indecision and personal suffering. Mme Ranevsky, who has traveled throughout Europe and might have been shown as a sophisticated woman of the world, is seen in all her impractical, emotional immaturity at a moment of pause in her frivolous life when she has to face herself and her past. In act 2, particularly, Chekov allowed each character to reveal himself within a mood that suggested that all rational processes had ceased, and subconscious longings had been allowed their full expression.

The dialogue of the play is difficult to define, because it is the ability of the actor interpreting the dialogue that makes it live and have meaning. The pauses, breaks, half-phrases, whispers, giggles, exclamations, tears, and laughter are as much a part of the dialogue as the words themselves. Chekov knew that the poetry of modern realism was to be found in those inarticulate moments when a human being is shown responding directly to his all too human situation. It is because Chekov said so little that he revealed so much.

Nothing could indicate more clearly the differences between *Ghosts* and *The Cherry Orchard* than the rhythms of the two plays. In *Ghosts,* the rhythm is tightly developed through incipient conflict to crisis to denouement, while in *The Cherry Orchard,* the rhythm is only loosely tied to three occasions: the return to the estate, its sale, and the final departure. Although the rhythm of *The Cherry Orchard* is subordinated to the emotional moods of the characters and the subtle poetry of the setting, it is one of the strongest values in the play—like the inexorable flow of an underground stream occasionally observed through an opening in the ground.

The play demands three realistic settings, two indoors and one outdoors. Although in its original production at the Moscow Art Theatre each setting was very literal, it should now be obvious that photographic fact in Chekov should be put aside in favor of suggestion. Lighting should be used indirectly to create a mood and atmosphere that is a balance between strict realism and symbolic impressionism. By Chekov's day, the symbolist movement in literature and the impressionist movement in art had reached full development, and much of the secondary level of effect in Chekov is impressionistic. Only by understanding how an impressionist painter would perceive light filtered through cherry blossoms, the sunset hours of a day, and a chandelier-illuminated party, can a designer have an appropriate feeling for the settings a production of *The Cherry Orchard* requires (Fig. 90).

The contrast between Ibsen and Chekov is reinforced by their use of furniture. Ibsen, like Degas, used furniture to strengthen conflict, control action, and focus movement and climax. Chekov, with his looser playwriting method, used furniture even more than Ibsen as symbols and reminders of the past to create a mood of events and feelings long forgotten. He also used furniture to underwrite the halting, broken rhythms of the play's development, as, for example, when he made Epihodov stumble over chairs.

The textures and colors used in the settings for *The Cherry Orchard* should appeal to a sense of association—to nostalgia for a past that is rapidly drifting away. The soft quality of tears, which continually erupt in act 3, must be reflected in the colors of the upholstery and draperies and in the soft lines of the furniture, paneling, and set decorations. All textural effects should help to establish the poetry behind the realistic plot, characters, and dialogue of the play. The poplar trees, which are the key to the visual mood of act 2, should have the mournful "dying fall" that will support the nostalgic and sad passage of time that is so important to this act, and the chandelier-lit party mood of the drawing room in act 3 should be created by a fading grandeur enclosing a sad happiness.

A study of the clothing in Renoir and Monet will be helpful to the designer in preparing costumes for *The Cherry Orchard*. Achieving some of the soft and vague effects of impressionism may seem difficult at first.

Figure 90
Act 1 of *The Cherry Orchard,* produced by The
American Conservatory Theatre, 1974, under the
direction of William Ball. Settings by Bob Blackman.
Costumes by Ann Roth. An example of simplified
realism to project mood through changes in lighting.
Courtesy American Conservatory Theatre, San
Francisco, California. Photo by Larry Kwart

Figure 91
Donald Moffat, Nancy Walker, and Uta Hagen in
The Cherry Orchard, produced by the APA-Phoenix
Repertory Company at the Lyceum Theater, New
York City, 1967. An example of the use of lace for
an impressionistic-realistic effect in costume. Cour-
tesy the APA-Phoenix Company. Photo by Van
Williams

Soft-textured woolens should be used for men's costumes. For women's costumes, fabrics with undefined patterns or whose surfaces change with the changing patterns of light should be used to create a sense of indefiniteness. Lace over solids will create the mottled and broken color effects of impressionism (Fig. 91).

The differences between *Ghosts* and *The Cherry Orchard* serve to underscore the range of realism in the theatre, which extends from strong plots and characterization that demand clear-cut sets and costumes, to a less obvious and far more subtle use of plot and characterization that demand more impressionistic sets and costumes.

8

Symbolist Theatre

To many artists and intellectuals, realism seemed to be a betrayal of the role of the artist in society and a debasement of art. The symbolist painters and poets who rejected realism as an answer to the challenge of modern industrial society were not late-blooming romantics but modernists who were probing beneath the surfaces of life and art. While the earlier romantics surrendered themselves to feeling to become emotionally involved in their art, the later romantics, who followed the lead of the poet Baudelaire, showed an unremitting concern for composition and style, and for turning the intuitive and the irrational into carefully planned artistic products. Art was seen as a movement, a shape, a rhythm to be imposed on feelings—a quite self-conscious attempt to impose personal style and form on the raw materials of life. Each artist hoped to ensure that his own stylistic view of experience would create a new, cohesive, cultural style that would reunite the artist with the great general public. Throughout the nineteenth century, when cultural absolutes were all but destroyed, the true artists, of whom the symbolists were only one group, were waging war against the false prestige and historical

Figure 92
Monet. *Rouen Cathedral,* 1894. An example of the dissolution of reality and structural form by mist and light in the later works of Monet. Mood, atmosphere, and a personal vision take precedence over visual facts. Courtesy The Metropolitan Museum of Art, The Theodore M. Davis Collection. Bequest of Theodore M. Davis, 1915

superficiality of the great academies and salons of art and literature. Finally, in the last decade of the century, certain artists developed and promoted a new style, art nouveau, which was the first great artistic movement in Europe since the Rococo.

In the symbolist movement, concentration was on form instead of content and on the inner life of material instead of the outward fact. The movement can be divided roughly into three submovements: (1) impressionistic symbolism, which stressed the inner secrets of life through mood and suggestion, (2) neomannerism, which stressed style and the manner of presentation instead of content; and (3) expressionistic symbolism, which depicted inner emotions through violent, harsh, and distorted attacks on the senses. All of the submovements turned their backs on reality and the objective facts of life and used symbols to make their artistic points.

Impressionistic symbolism was an art of suggestion, in which the early symbolist poets and painters used vague and impressionistic symbols to suggest deeply buried inner feelings. Even impressionistic painting, originally intended to expand optical reality through the creation of momentary effect, gradually changed in the work of Monet, for example, into vague, moody, dreamlike painting whose effects were often close to the sublimated reveries of the symbolist poets (Fig. 92). The ideal of the impressionistic symbolists was that art be like the memory of music that has passed away. The painter Redon came closest to this ideal in his works entitled *Silence, The Thought,* and *The Dream.* He used the resources of the inner mind, not the world of the senses, to develop his images, and his hope was to create a painting that conveyed the uncertainty and indefiniteness of mood that was formerly possible to convey only in music (Fig. 93). In drama this method was followed by Maurice Maeterlinck, whose play *Pelléas et Mélisande,* came to full realization only when Claude Debussy, who was the great exponent of the impressionist tradition in music, made this drama into an opera. In Debussy's vague, moody, shifting evocations of the forest, the moon, and the sea we have in music what the painters and poets longed for in their art.

Figure 93
Redon. *Reverie,* ca. 1900. An example of the mystery in symbolist painting. Redon hoped to "put the logic of the visible at the service of the invisible." Courtesy Collection, The Museum of Modern Art, New York. Gift of Abby Aldrich Rockefeller

But impressionistic symbolism tended to be formless and it was to this problem that the neomannerists addressed themselves. They used many of the same images and symbols as the impressionistic symbolists, but stressed form, design, and pattern as well as mood. They developed artificiality and style almost as an end in itself, in much the same way as the sixteenth century mannerists did. For example, in Gauguin's *The Day of the God,* the flat poster, the woodcut, and the Japanese print were as important in shaping the decorative pattern of the composition as South Seas mythology was in shaping the content and mood (Fig. 94).

The beginnings of expressionistic symbolism became apparent in the 1890's in the paintings of Munch, Ensor, and Van Gogh and in the plays of August Strindberg. Their artistic products reflected the very subjective developments that neurotic and tortured personalities undergo in a modern, industrial, bourgeois society (Fig. 95). Patterns and symbols depicting the outer world through the inner world of the artist were used in a distorted, explosive, violent, and nightmarish manner. In its attacks on the sufferings, horrors, and injustices of life, expressionistic symbolist art produced results that were often distorted to near abstraction; this led eventually to the abstract expressionist movement following World War II.

The symbolist movement in the theatre had its origins as early as the middle of the nineteenth century in the theories of Richard Wagner, who dedicated himself to a fusion of music, dialogue, color, light, shape, and texture that would give a unified theatrical mood. In his theater at Bayreuth, Wagner used a double proscenium, a curtain of steam, and a darkened auditorium to create a mystic division between audience and stage that would allow spectators to lose themselves in the artistic magic of the production. Men of the symbolist theatre, such as Paul Fort and Aurélien-Marie Lugné-Poë, borrowed many of Wagner's precepts when they premiered Maeterlinck's *Pelléas et Mélisande* at the Théâtre l'Oeuvre in 1892 with a transparent curtain in front of the action and a great stress on mood. At about the same time, Adolphe Appia, in an effort to bring

Figure 94

Gauguin. *The Day of the God,* 1894. An example of creating a strong sense of mood and style through pattern that made Gauguin a leader among the symbolists as well as among the artists of Art Nouveau. Courtesy The Art Institute of Chicago

the ideals of Wagner to fruition, developed stage lighting as the great unifying factor in a production. Appia used lighting to define the actor in space against simple, abstract, three-dimensional forms and to support the continually shifting moods in action and music (Fig. 96).

A few years later the young English designer Gordon Craig not only further developed and lobbied for these Wagnerian and Appian ideals, but he also placed more emphasis than had Wagner and Appia on the superartist-director, who blended actions, words, lines, colors, and rhythms into a great artistic work, where the script was only a part of a much larger whole (Fig. 97).

The influence of Appia and Craig was immense and could be seen in most artistically designed productions prior to World War I. The scenic precepts of the symbolists might be condensed as follows: There was to be a simplification of means and effect; an appropriate relationship of actor to background; simple suggestion, by which a single candelabrum might symbolize the culture of the Baroque era; and a synthesis of all elements of a production into a complex and rhythmic fusion of sets, costumes, lights, actors, and script.

The theatre artist who best transformed these symbolist precepts into exciting theatrical productions was Max Reinhardt, who took Craig's slogan, "Not realism, but style," coupled it to the concept of director as master theatre artist and seer, and gave a new meaning throughout Europe to the title *regisseur*. Reinhardt paraded before the public the theatrical styles of the past and of the Orient in great eclectic revivals that used visual and aural symbols to give unity in production. Although his eclecticism was criticized by the modernists, he did bring the visual arts back into the theatre (Fig. 98). He became the master showman of the new theatre, and his name became a household word in both the United States and Europe. American artist-designers, such as Robert Edmond Jones, Lee Simonson, Donald Oenslager, Norman Bel Geddes, and Jo Mielziner, carried the ideals of Appia, Craig, and Reinhardt into the exciting era of American theatre that followed World War I (Fig. 99).

Figure 95
Munch. *The Scream,* 1893. An example of the swirling brushstrokes, harsh color, and exaggerated shapes that carry the artist's subjective and overpowering image of fear to the level of nightmare. Courtesy National Gallery, Oslo, Norway

Figure 96
Design for *Parsifal* by Adolphe Appia, 1896. An example of Appia's principle that scenery and lighting must be designed to express and heighten the playwright's intention at each moment in a play or opera. From G. Altman et al., *Theater Pictorial.* Courtesy William Melnitz

Figure 97
An original sketch for an ideal theater, by Gordon Craig, ca. 1908. An example of the simple and magnificent forms given mood and beauty through dramatic lighting effects that marked the work of the new stagecraft and the arrival of symbolism in theatrical design. Courtesy Norman Philbrick Library

LIMELIGHTS
WORKED FROM
3 GALLERIES
SUSPENDED
FROM THE ROOF

ORCHESTRA

ENTRANCE
& EXIT

ENTRANCE
FOR PERFORMERS

EXIT

GREAT
BACKCLOTH
USED WHEN
THE DOORS
ARE THROWN
OPEN

SECTION TAKEN
OUT OF FLOORING TO
SHOW THE UNDERGROUND
ARRANGEMENTS TO RAISE AND
LOWER STAGE

POSITION OF
HILL AND TREES
WHEN IN THE
ARENA

LESSER
SLIDING-DOOR
WHICH FITS
INTO THE
GREAT
DOOR

RAILS ON WHICH
THE HILL AND
TREES MOVES INTO
THE ARENA

GREAT SLIDING
DOOR

PLAYERS
MAKING
READY
IN THE
CORRIDORS

Symbolist Theatre

176

Figure 98
A scene from *The Miracle,* produced by Max Reinhardt at the Olympia Theatre, London, 1911. An example of the spectacular, style-conscious productions of this master of artistic eclecticism. Courtesy Victoria and Albert Museum, Crown Copyright

Figure 99
A sketch for act 3, scene 4 of Shakespeare's *Macbeth* as designed by Robert Edmond Jones for a production at the Apollo Theatre, New York City, produced and directed by Arthur Hopkins, 1921. An example of violent theatrical expressionism used in presenting the psychology of the protagonist. From Ralph Pendleton, ed., *The Theatre of Robert Edmond Jones* (1958). Courtesy Mrs. Honor Leeming Luttgen Collection

One of the most fully symbolic dramas written to exemplify the precepts of impressionistic symbolism was Maeterlinck's *Pelléas et Mélisande*. In many ways the moody tale cried out for music, and it was a perfect wedding of composer and author when Debussy made the play into an opera in 1902 (Fig. 100). Based on Dante's tale of Paolo and Francesca, the structural development of Maeterlinck's *Pelléas et Mélisande* consists of a series of loosely connected scenes showing the tragic love affair of the two protagonists. Each scene is based on some mood-evoking symbol: at one point Mélisande's doves leave her forever; at another she loses the ring that symbolizes her marriage vow; and at another, Yniold tries to lift a stone that symbolizes the weight of sin fallen on his family. It is mood and theme that count; the number of scenes in the play could be expanded or reduced without much effect on the development of the story. The scenes are connected by a pervasive symbolic atmosphere rather than by a cause-and-effect chain of events.

The characters in the play are as vague and mysterious as the mood. They embody shadowy feelings and desires that yearn for enlightenment, yet they are destined to live and die, governed by some inexplicable fate. About all we know about the characters is their age, social class, and names; their personalities are only vaguely suggested. Fate is the great life force that hangs over all the characters. Maeterlinck was not interested in three-dimensional, flesh-and-blood people, but in states of mind that crept up on his characters mysteriously and led to inscrutable consequences.

Maeterlinck used repeated motifs and symbols to support his theme that fate governs all. Water occurs over and over again as a symbol of the mysteries of life: There is the pool where Mélisande is first discovered; the fountain in which she loses her ring; the bottomless pits of water under the castle; the water used to wash the blood stains from the steps; and the sea, which is a soul-beckoning place of release. The same kind of repetition occurs with darkness and light: the forests are ever

Figure 100
A scene from *Pelléas et Mélisande* by Maeterlinck and Debussy, produced at the San Francisco Opera, San Francisco, 1965. An example of a few simple set pieces used as symbols to be picked out by dramatic lighting to achieve the mood and impressions required. Courtesy San Francisco Opera, San Francisco, California. Photo by Pete Peters

dark; the characters are seated in darkness groping toward light; and lamps die out and cannot be relit. Throughout the play, love, happiness, and light are in a continuous struggle with fate and the forces of darkness. Maeterlinck was obsessed with an even more deterministic philosophy than the realists and naturalists; he saw all life as a mysterious and impenetrable unknown.

Maeterlinck made the language of his play extremely simple and repetitive so that words and phrases would ring in the ear as symbols of ineffable feelings. In his long essay, *The Treasure of the Humble,* Maeterlinck described a second level of language, the dialogue "for the soul," where seemingly unnecessary and superfluous words and phrases speak to man's deepest strivings toward beauty and truth. The playwright expected his audience to search behind the words and the pauses within sentences for the play's ultimate significance. The rhythm of the play, closely tied to the use of words, is gentle, shifting, somewhat vague, and without abrupt changes like the moods and rhythms of quiet, flowing music.

The demands for appropriate visual presentation are very insistent in this play even though specific effects are vague and elusive. In the original production of *Pelléas et Mélisande* the stage lighting was from overhead and low in intensity, and a gauze curtain hung at the front of the stage to keep the action misty and at a distance. The scenery and costumes were designed in pale gray tones and the movement and gestures were unreal and trancelike—as if bodies and limbs were moved by some unseen force. The keys to a successful production of this play are the word *mist* and the use of light (Fig. 101).

Today it is unlikely that this play would be revived, because we are all involved in a continuing reaction against the vagueness of symbolist style. The opera *Pelléas et Mélisande* is frequently performed, but even in it contemporary producers usually try to appeal more directly to the

Figure 101
A sketch for act 4, scene 3 of *Pelléas et Mélisande* by Maeterlinck and Debussy, designed by Robert Edmond Jones as a project, 1921. A further example of simple forms used in an impressionistic way to achieve mood and mystery. From Pendleton, *The Theatre of Robert Edmond Jones.* Courtesy Yale School of Drama Print Collection

Symbolist Theatre

182

senses rather than create a vagueness and trancelike reverie. The problem with impressionistic symbolism is its lack of concrete, clear-cut meaning. Therefore, the producer of a contemporary production of *Pelléas et Mélisande* must concentrate less on vagueness and suggestion and more on strong mood and atmosphere. Curtains between scenes should be removed; there should be a continuous flow of action from scene to scene, supported and brought into focus by lighting. The shifting of set pieces should be as simple as possible to avoid interrupting the play's rhythm and audience concentration. Simple shapes and forms, with a stress on sensuous textures, should be used to suggest the various locales within the play and the entire action should be orchestrated by light and developed as if part of a musical composition. Sharp, bleak rocks, jagged branches against a dying sky, heavy, shadowed castle stones lost in a veil of mist—each specific image must be simple without the clutter of atmospheric detail that marked symbolist production in the early twentieth century. The pattern of movement within the setting should be close to that of a ballet or dance—choreographed to achieve a vague, floating, musical effect that is the essence of this play. Acting and gestures should be part of the total mood rather than individual characterization. Textures within the setting should be soft, vague, and light absorbing, without sharp, harsh details. Color, if it is used in the setting, should be soft and gray, not hard and brilliant, and able to be transformed subtly by lighting. All lines and shapes within the setting should be developed to give a maximum impact on the senses and the fullest stress on the symbols of the play with a minimum of means (Fig. 102).

The costumes for *Pelléas et Mélisande* are difficult because they must suggest rather than state; the audience should not recognize them as period clothing. Instead, costumes should recall a generalized, vague, unspecified time in the past, with concentration on the subtle, abstract, mood effects of color, texture, line, and movement rather than on period detail. Early medieval sources, with their flowing, draped lines, rather than fourteenth or fifteenth century sources, with their stress on pattern,

Figure 102
A scene from *Pelléas et Mélisande* by Maeterlinck, produced by the Belgian National Theatre, 1963. An example of indefinite, mood-producing forms, soft, draped lines, and shiny textures in costume used to create an impression through atmosphere. Courtesy Belgian National Theatre. Photo by Carl Hensler

ornament, and rich accessories, should provide examples for the general lines of the costumes. Since simplicity and vagueness are essential in capturing the mood and unreality of the play, the costume fabrics should probably be changeable materials, chiffons, gauzes, Chinese silks, and soft woolens and piles. Layers of filmy fabric can be used over shimmering metallics to gain a sense of richness and depth.

Because of its lack of concrete effects, impressionistic symbolism appealed to a limited audience. Although the movement produced few important and lasting plays, its technique of design had a strong influence on the theatre. Its inheritance is still strong today.

The upheavals brought about by World War I, and the great influence of the machine and Freudian psychology on man's thinking, produced the symbolist submovement known as expressionistic symbolism. *From Morn to Midnight,* written by the German dramatist Georg Kaiser before World War I and produced for the first time in 1917, stands as a clear-cut example of the style. While it retained the personal, subjective vision of symbolism, it lashed out in a direct assault on audience sensibilities and depicted a world twisted and distorted by inhuman values.

The play was written in scenes rather than acts, using the idea of the morality play to depict the end of modern man in seven steps. The time from morn to midnight is the Cashier's journey from birth to death, and, like Oedipus, Faust, and Mrs. Alving, his search is for personal fulfillment—a quest that ends not in hope but in the debasement of modern man. Unity comes not from any logical organization of the scenes or from causally related events, but from an illumination of the play's theme by concentrating on the psychological deterioration of the Cashier as Everyman. In the beginning, as a fugitive from the bank and normal society, the Cashier thinks he will find an answer to life through his stolen money, his new-found freedom, and his willingness to explore all of life's possibilities. But he soon meets death for the first time, and in subsequent scenes he can find no answers in family, politics, money, sensual pleasure, or religion. His final disillusionment comes when the

Salvation Army girl who pretended to be interested in his soul turns him over to the police for a reward. At the end of the play a tangle of wires outlines the form of death. As the Cashier runs into the wires with arms outstretched like Christ upon the cross, there is a great crackling of electricity and an exploding of lamps. The ultimate comment is given by the policeman who says, "There seems to be a short circuit in the wiring."

Each of the characters in *From Morn to Midnight* is given a label, not a name, and each acts as a kind of mechanical robot in projecting Kaiser's mechanistic view of modern life. Only the lady from Italy, who represents an older way of life, and the Cashier, who symbolizes the search for a new way of life, escape the mechanistic pattern to some extent. The Cashier is, of course, the spokesman for the playwright and therefore the only character who senses that there must be an escape from the machinelike existence of modern society. Although the Cashier deepens his understanding of his relationship to society as the play progresses, he never becomes a full, three-dimensional character. He must remain more a symbol than an individual personality.

The theme of *From Morn to Midnight* is that the mechanistic ideals of modern life must be changed. Although the play ends on a note of pessimism, it does suggest that a new man may emerge from the soulless automaton that is modern man and that mankind may be redeemed. The language of the play is developed along mechanistic lines with the intention of presenting quick, staccato patterns that reflect the violent, short-circuited, direct impulses of communications transmitted by machine. Kaiser used language that was frequently repetitious, heightened in volume, forced in pace, and harsh in effect to achieve the maximum in aggressive attack on the audience. The rhythm of the play is strong and insistent in its mechanistic drive. With its violent shifts from moment to moment, it allows little sense of rest and relaxation. Its beat is one of the most powerful means in the play for stressing the mechanized, inhuman feelings the playwright wishes to express.

The third scene of the play provides the strongest clue for the design concept: the tree must turn into a skeleton before the eyes of the audience, and this same sense of visual distortion is needed in the other six scenes of the play. In this way, only the Cashier and the audience perceive the true reality underneath the surface of modern life. The other characters presumably see everything as normal, while the "awakened" Cashier sees life as it is. In the original productions of expressionist dramas in the period between World Wars I and II, great use was made of cubistic, distorted forms, tilted angles, and exaggerated or diminished size. Color was also unnatural and great attention was given to exaggerated and violent effects in the stage lighting (Fig. 103). In the complex, unsentimental, nonidealistic world of today, it might be difficult to revive *From Morn to Midnight* in a direct way because of its naïve simplicity, but if great stress were placed in its production on the contemporary sensual, visual, and motion effects found in rock musicals, light shows, welded sculpture, and junk art, the play's message might seem as immediate as that in many popular songs.

The mechanistic quality of the designs for *From Morn to Midnight* might reflect either the smooth, riveted, machine-tooled, colorless surfaces that we find in industrial machinery, or the corroded, broken, decaying forms found in junk yards and dumps or in the wastebins of modern industry. The first approach would be effective in the mechanized scenes at the race track and the bank; the second, in both the third scene, where Death appears in the gnarled tree, and the last scene, where the Cashier runs into the tangled wires of death. No matter what the source for the colors, textures, and lines of the settings may be, the lighting must act as the major unifying and projecting device of the play. The methods of modern "light shows," such as spiraling, swirling, and bursting color, could be used with brilliant effect to support the emotional climate of each scene. The use of electronic music would also support the play's mood of mechanization.

The mechanical qualities of the settings, lighting, and music should be reflected in the costumes. If a smooth, polished, mechanistic approach

Figure 103
A scene from *From Morn to Midnight* by Georg Kaiser, produced at the Lessing Theater, West Berlin. Courtesy Picture Archives, Austrian National Library

is used, then the costumes should reflect the metallic, plastic, manufactured look of space suits. If a decaying, corroded approach is used, then melted nylon, burned sponge rubber, and acid-eaten plastics, painted to further the effect of decomposing surfaces, would be effective in indicating the final end for mechanized man.

The history of expressionism may be limited, but the emotional effects engendered in the movement can easily be updated for modern production. Many plays from the past can be presented to modern audiences in a neo-expressionist manner that will fit exactly the mood of much contemporary theatre and effectively communicate a modern point from a script that would otherwise lack relevance when presented in a straightforward period manner.

9

Relativist Theatre

The symbolist movement finally reached a crisis point in the early years of the twentieth century because of its excessive stress on the subjective in art. Nineteenth century artists, from Turner and Delacroix to Munch and Van Gogh, were unable or unwilling to use the methods of science intelligently in their art. Impressionist painters, who began with a scientific interest in optics and light, drifted into moodiness and subjectivism, and dramatists of realistic theatre, such as Ibsen and Chekov, who began with an interest in the scientific probing of the current social scene, shifted into symbolism in their later plays. What was needed was a new stress on complex intellectual ideas and rationality of form rather than an emphasis on mood and the psychology of the unconscious. This was not to arrive in the theatre until Luigi Pirandello made the philosophic idea the center of drama. Even in music and poetry, artists were unwilling to analyze scientifically the nature of their media, to open it up to new experiments in form. The only science that aroused some response from nineteenth century artists was Darwinian biology, a discipline which seemed to sanction, however, strong animal instincts and subjective impulses rather than intelligence. Art and science had become alienated during this period and no major attempts were made to relate the new discoveries in science to the world of art. Artists in all media therefore suffered from the lack of a firm intellectual base for their art. The sculpture of Rodin, for example, was dynamic, energetic, theatrical, and highly emotional, but it lacked intellectual conception. Rodin's vagueness was reminiscent of Maeterlinck, his strength and mass, of Michelangelo; what was lacking was a concept of simultaneous space—a succession of moments perceived in a single space-time continuum. The energy and tension of Rodin's sculpture was a manifestation of the artist's rebellion against the static qualities of three-dimensional space. Although Rodin was a powerful and theatrical sculptor, he never found a substitute sculptural structure (Fig. 104).

The great innovator of the late nineteenth century was the French painter Cézanne, who was determined to bring to impressionism the solidity and intellectual foundation of classical art. He worked slowly until his death in 1906 on still lifes and views of Mont Sainte Victoire to elicit a carefully built structure from the piling-up of blocks and spots of color and value, and to take the momentary perception and make it into a long and analytical view of the inner and outer structure of his subject (Fig. 105).

Within a year or two of Cézanne's death, Picasso and Braque began to experiment with cubism. They went a step further than Cézanne and dismembered the geometric relationships of the real world and reorganized them to be viewed with the mind as well as with the eye. Unlike the symbolists, who distorted life for emotional effect, the cubists and other abstractionists took things apart in a semiscientific way to see how they worked, and then reconstituted them to show simultaneously their inner and outer dynamics. The concept of the simultaneous perception of several separate views of reality evolved at a time when science was in the process of promulgating the theory of relativity, which implied that even the laws of science were mutable and changing—that the nature of reality was based on flux and change (Fig. 106).

Figure 104
Rodin. *The Gates of Hell,* ca. 1880. An example of impressionistic rather than structural vision in architectural sculpture. Courtesy Musée Rodin, Paris

191

Figure 105
Cézanne. *Mont Sainte Victoire,* ca. 1905. An example
of how Cézanne tried to structure and organize
impressionist art to give it the solidity of classical
art. Courtesy Philadelphia Museum of Art, The
George W. Elkins Collection

Figure 106
Moore. *Internal and External Forms,* 1953–1954. An
example of the interpenetration of space and form
to create a number of changing levels of reality.
Courtesy of the Albright-Knox Art Gallery, Buffalo,
New York, Consolidated Purchase Funds

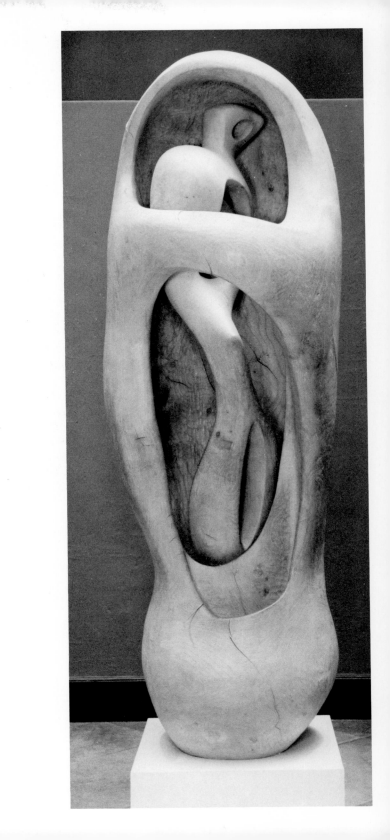

The new art differed sharply from nineteenth century art, in fact, from all art since the time of Giotto, because it stressed how the artist thought rather than how he saw. It was an intellectual, scientific, organizational art that was a projection of the way in which man analyzed and pondered what he saw. The new art form was the collage, in which the problems of construction in a painting were projected. Real objects and textures were juxtaposed with painted effects to underline points of intersection between various levels of reality. The collage served as a kind of diagram of the shifting realities and perspectives of life.

The final result of the cubists' experimentation with reality was the eventual liberation of art from subject. With abstract expressionists like Jackson Pollock this meant that the artist had a physical relationship with his work in the dribbling and spurting of pigment onto canvas. Thus the texture of the field became more important than the objects in the field (Fig. 107). With neoplasticists like Mondrian this meant working with the most pure and simplified colors and geometric forms to gain the most perfect relationships without reference to the real world (see Fig. 13).

The exhausted conclusion of the cubist and abstract expressionist movements came in the early 1960s with op and pop art and the "aliterature" of Alain Robbe-Grillet. Op and pop artists and writers of the period denied the complexities of the culture, had no strong point of view, and merely recorded certain physical facts and relationships.

In the theatre, the acceptance of and the willingness to experiment with multiple reality came slowly. It was not until Pirandello's *Six Characters in Search of an Author* was produced in 1923 that the new direction in art seemed fully accepted into the drama. Earlier movements in theatre production, however, had shown a subtle, almost imperceptible motion toward the concept of multiple reality. The first step was the break with illusionism and the picture-window view of a performance in favor of a return to the Elizabethan idea of the stage as a platform for performance. The Elizabethan Stage Society in England, under the idealist and reformer

Figure 107
Pollock. *Autumn Rhythm*, 1950. An example of free-form action painting in which texture rather than a defined pattern is created. Nature is reduced to the movement of forces in a field. Courtesy The Metropolitan Museum of Art, George A. Hearn Fund, 1957

Relativist Theatre

195

William Poel, insisted on a return to Elizabethan staging methods for Elizabethan plays to gain a sense of immediacy, swift flow of action, and direct storytelling without illusionistic accoutrements. Just prior to World War I, at the Vieux Columbier in Paris, Jacques Copeau further developed the idea of a permanent, formal stage (Fig. 108). Experiments carried on in Germany by Max Reinhardt led to a return of the Greek orchestra and the thrusting of acting into the audience, such as occurred at performances at the Circus Schumann and the Grosses Schauspielhaus in Berlin. There were also attempts to return to the simultaneous staging of medieval theatre, where all scenes were set before the audience as they entered the theater.

These experiments with a double reality, that is, the formal stage and the fictional play, were tame in comparison with the wild experiments in constructivism carried out in Russian theatre after World War I. Constructivist theatre, in which all plays were presented as strong social statements in the service of the new proletarian state, used a severely limited play script as a libretto for physical action that expressed the rhythm, tempo, and emotional structure of the play. Actors were trained in a system called *biomechanics* to become instruments of movement in the hands of the master director, and stress was laid on ballet, acrobatics, gymnastics, and group movement rather than on any psychological interpretation of character. The setting became a machine for action—a construction in space upon which actors could work like the rhythmic parts of moving machinery (Fig. 109). Here was the sharpest intellectual distinction to date between the physical reality of the actor and the reality of his role, between the audience's world of reality and the reality placed upon the stage. It was in many ways the first use of the multiple realities of cubism in the theatre—the first use of the intellectual concepts of relativity and abstraction.

Probably the most influential use of the new relativist concepts came with the epic theatre productions of the plays of Berthold Brecht and

Figure 108
A setting for Le Théâtre du Vieux Colombier, Paris, ca. 1913. An example of the use of a basic architectural stage, developed by Jacques Copeau. The stage remained part of the auditorium and was changed by the minor use of props and set pieces. From *Continental Stagecraft*, by Kenneth Macgowan and Robert E. Jones. Courtesy Harcourt Brace Jovanovich, Inc., publishers.

Relativist Theatre

Relativist Theatre

198

Erwin Piscator. Their plays were presented as great, unrolling narratives, using various media such as songs, slides, movies, signs, and other special properties to support the actors in their presentation of ever-changing views and angles of reality. The response of the audience to this kind of interpretation was meant to be intellectual rather than emotional, critical rather than sentimental. Brecht chose far-away settings, historical subjects, and somewhat strange tales for his dramatizations to remove or alienate his audience from direct emotional involvement and thus lead them into thinking about social problems rather than losing themselves in emotional identifications with his characters.

Finally, as a culminating movement in the 1950s, came the phenomenon of absurdism, which was at first a philosophy of playwriting but rapidly became a method of production. In an attempt to portray the meaninglessness and absurdity of everyday existence, expressionist exaggerations, normal bourgeois properties, and symbolic bits and pieces from everyday society were mixed together and jostled against each other within an intellectual collage of words and ideas presented by characters who had no single reality. Absurdist plays tended to be intellectual games played with the pieces of fragmented modern reality, and they carried the pessimistic moral that all life is totally without meaning.

Let us look briefly at three twentieth century plays and the different ways in which each play exemplified relativist method.

Luigi Pirandello's *Six Characters in Search of an Author* was the definitive drama that marked the emergence of twentieth century playwriting from late nineteenth century realism and symbolism. As Wylie Sypher points out in *Rococo to Cubism in Art and Literature, Six Characters* was the first cubist drama—a play in which the stage was a plane for the intersection of art and life, a place for the collision between art and reality. Plot in the usual sense is missing as the audience is expected to move from a concentration on the realities of a stage rehearsal to events in the lives of characters only partially drawn by an unknown author. By refusing the movement and forward thrust of plot, Pirandello was left with the formal artistic problem of writing a drama about a drama. His technique

Figure 109
Stage setting for *The Magnificent Cuckold* by Crommelynck, produced by Vsevolod Meyerhold in 1922. An example of constructivism. The setting became a structure for organizing action and space on a platform in front of an audience. Courtesy Soviet Bureau of Cultural Affairs, Washington, D.C.

in working out this problem was similar to the visual technique of collage developed by the cubists. In fact, the strongest connection between *Six Characters* (and the many plays that derive from it) and the visual arts is the collage. Pirandello pieced together and arranged a number of theatrical clichés to form a collage of intermingling and interpenetrating realities: the attitudes of the director, the concepts of commercial theatre, the outlook of the professional actor, the contributions of stagehands, the method of a missing playwright, and a group of partially realized characters. The six "characters" belong to life and yet they do not belong. Pirandello stopped the film of their lives at a crucial episode that must be replayed forever, while the actors, the director, and even the audience argue over the nature of reality. Thus all characters in the play are realistic on their own level, but their reality is brought into question when pitted against other levels of reality.

Every moment of the play points up and exemplifies the thesis that reality is a shifting thing and, at times, the reality of art and imitation may be greater than the reality of life. As the actors and director argue about the nature of reality with the "characters," the dialogue shifts from real-life conversation to rational argument to theatrical clichés, without transition or warning, to demonstrate the multiple levels of reality. The rhythm of the play is closest to that of the experimental film, where the camera can make a story go backward or forward, dissolve into multiple images, or undergo a reality change. Pirandello made his play stop, start, shift abruptly, and change levels without warning in an attempt to frustrate an easy acceptance of sequence and forward movement.

The visual demands for production consciously take on the aspect of collage, as bits and pieces of costume and scenery are collected to create Mme. Pacé's "establishment" (Fig. 110). The backstage realities of bare walls, props, set pieces, and costume racks merge with and are used by the six "characters" in presenting their story. The result is an intersection of theatrical reality, life reality, and "character" reality.

Figure 110
A scene from *Six Characters in Search of an Author* by Pirandello, produced by The American Conservatory Theatre for the Stanford Summer Festival, 1966. An example of multiple reality in which a scene was constructed in front of the audience from backstage properties and set pieces. Courtesy American Conservatory Theatre, San Francisco, California. Photo by Hank Kranzler

Relativist Theatre

202

Since Pirandello's playwriting method was intellectually rich but visually spare, the visual choices for a contemporary production must be carefully selected to project the intellectual shifts in the argument without creating emotionally or sensuously distracting effects (Fig. 111). Visually exciting effects should be used to highlight a basically lean production. The ritual of the actors arriving for rehearsal can be made into a visually interesting charade; the arrival of the "characters" can be made very theatrical by an eerie light playing on their pale faces; and the readying of the white parlor can be made into a dramatic moment by using floral decoration as a backing for the "characters'" story. The strongest visual incident in the play is the appearance of Mme. Pacé, who should move, as if by transmigration from another world, into a collage erected to represent her establishment. Lighting is very important in all of these episodes, as is a strong contrast in the use of make-up, costumes, properties, and scenery—a contrast of one reality placed within the frame of another. Any visual effects will become meaningless unless the philosophical framework within which the play operates is kept in sharp focus before the audience at all times. In all matters of setting and costume the problem is one of selection rather than design. For a collage or an assemblage, the visual elements must be carefully chosen, placed exactly within the action, and used at a prescribed moment in a specified way.

While Pirandello used the stage and theatrical "characters" as a means of calling into question the nature of reality, Brecht used the effects of the multiple reality of actor, character, and audience—of platform, place, and auditorium—to comment on modern society. Although he used a more sensory and more complicated visual statement to arouse the interest and attention of his audience, he encouraged intellectual, critical comment rather than emotional response from his public.

In *The Goodwoman of Setzuan*, which was first produced in Switzerland in 1943, Brecht used a parable form to tell his story, and removed the

Figure 111
A scene from *Six Characters in Search of an Author* by Pirandello, produced by The Stanford Players, Stanford University, 1951. An example of the importance of the stage as a stage and the actor as an actor in this seminal drama dealing with the concept that truth is merely a matter of one's point of view.
Courtesy Stanford University Archives

events from the European scene by placing the action in China. The narrative or epic structure of the play is established by the prologue, which mingles dialogue and narration and compresses information about time and place to establish the basic situation from which the play will begin. The play then progresses through alternating long and short scenes, the long ones projecting the action forward, the short ones breaking it up with comment and discussion. Brecht inserted songs, speeches to the audience, and filmed sequences to comment upon the action. He had little concern for psychological truth, and felt that the social commentary of each scene could be summarized by one simple declarative sentence. Although Brecht's technique aimed at simplicity and clarity, it often confused an audience looking for clear transitions and obvious motivations. If the play is accepted as a fable or parable, however, Brecht's method can be successful.

Brecht deliberately oversimplified his characters to project their social and economic relationships. Many of the characters do not have names, but social labels, such as gods, Wife, Carpenter, Policeman, and Old Man. The social behavior of the characters is the key in *The Goodwoman of Setzuan,* not their individual and personal motivations. Only Shen Te, the heroine, rises to the level of personal moral decision, which is forced on her by the economic system. At first Shen Te accepts the gods' admonition to be good, but then shifts to a disguise as the evil Shui Ta to preserve herself and her man, Yang Sung.

Shen Te's choice between good and evil represents the moral dilemma that Brecht saw confronting all people experiencing the economic conditions of western capitalism. Although Brecht implies that capitalism is destructive to human nature, he indicts not only the capitalists but also the working class for their callousness to human suffering, and we are left to feel that, regardless of the economic system, human nature will be selfish and exploitive. Thus there is a certain ambiguity in the play: a sense of optimism about the possibility for social change and a sense of pessimism and hopelessness about the human condition.

The language of the play is varied. Straightforward character dialogue, narrative-descriptive speech, direct critical comment, short bits of symbolic verse, and song are used to underline the play's basic theme. The song "The Water Seller in the Rain," sung by Wong, is not only a breathing point in the narrative and a humorous comment on Wong and his profession, but also a cynical and bitter attempt to contrast rain, which is free, with water, which is sold.

The play's rhythm, which is like a series of improvisations or charades, comes from Brecht's experience with cabaret entertainment. It is a broken rhythm like that found in a planned evening of song, dance, comment, and dramatization on a single theme.

The visual requirements of Brechtian drama are also comprised of many separate items that can be easily organized into varying realities by the actors during an evening's entertainment. Brecht wanted the visual elements of his play to be free from pictorial illusionism and to project a childlike naïveté—a simple make-believe created with fragmentary sets, properties, and costumes, bright circus lights, and musicians on stage. *The Goodwoman of Setzuan*, which is set in ten different places, can be staged with a very few scenic elements. A mobile arrangement of flats and platforms can be pushed and pulled and turned around by the actors to suggest a number of locations. Properties, set pieces, signs, posters, projections, and films can be added or subtracted during the course of the action. Such a setting may at first appear to be inartistic, a mere piling up of findings from storerooms and secondhand stores, but it is the arrangement and selection of these findings to support the action and intellectual comment of the play that challenges the designer's skill. When Kurt Schwitter's *Merz* constructions first appeared in Germany after World War I, they were too frequently thought of as nonart, but became the forerunners of so-called junk art, a legitimate part of modern art (Fig. 112). A Brechtian set may look like junk art, but if it works effectively to project the play it is a success.

The pseudo-Chinese setting for *The Goodwoman of Setzuan* may suggest the shapes and textures of shipping crates, lanterns, corrugated metal, bamboo, paper screens, burlap, and choice items from the junk shop or antique store—all used in a childlike, make-believe way to support and comment on the play (Fig. 113).

Figure 112
Schwitters. *Merz Construction* (painted wood, wire,
and paper), 1921. An example of so-called trash
art, which attempted to make interesting abstract
arrangements of elements taken from a number
of levels of reality. Such art was very influential
in stage design. Courtesy Philadelphia Museum
of Art, The A. E. Gallatin Collection

Figure 113
A scene from *The Goodwoman of Setzuan* by Brecht,
produced by The Stanford Repertory Theatre, Stanford University, 1966. An example of "the epic
theatre," in which action was kept "theatrical," the
mechanics of the play remained visible, and the
story was presented or told through narration and
action rather than completely dramatized. Photo by
Hank Kranzler, San Francisco, California

The costumes should look like clothing selected from a wardrobe or secondhand store. They should suggest character, comment on action, and indicate the pseudo-Chinese setting of the play, but should never contribute to unity of visual effect. While the costumes should communicate the reality or information required at a given moment, the audience must always think of them as theatrical "dress-ups" for the occasion (Fig. 114).

One of the most complex examples of the use of multiple reality in the theatre is Jean Genêt's *The Blacks.* The play creates a bizarre and confusing picture of the shifting realities confronting modern man—man caught in a maze of mirrors, trapped by the reflections of his distorted image, trying to make contact with those around him but rudely stopped by the barriers created by the reflecting glass. In *The Blacks,* which Genêt called a clown show, a group of blacks playing both black and white roles reenacts a ritualistic revenge on the white man's world. There is no story line or clearly developed plot. The cast is divided into those who enact the black man's fantasy of himself and those who enact the black man's fantasy about white reaction to the black world. Thus black actors stand between an audience (ideally composed of white people) and the white-masked, colonial, fantasy audience composed of the haughty Queen, the Judge, the Bishop, the Governor-General, and the Valet, who acts the part of the artist-intellectual. In front of this hierarchy of white power, the other group of blacks acts out its fantasies of resentment in an elaborately detailed ritual murder of a white woman. Archibald, the stage manager or master of ceremonies, makes it clear that the action onstage is a make-believe ritual, and that the evening's entertainment is meant to overawe and mystify the audience rather than involve them in conceptual or rational communication. By the end of the evening another reality erupts upon the stage when a young man sent off earlier with a gun returns to report an offstage revolt. The ritual murder onstage suddenly appears to have been a blind, a diversionary tactic used to distract

Figure 114
Costume sketches for Wong and the Three Gods, by Richard L. Hay, for *The Goodwoman of Setzuan* by Brecht, produced by The Stanford Repertory Theatre, Stanford University, 1966. An example of the stress on texture and comic comment that is called for in the costumes for a Brechtian production. Courtesy Richard L. Hay

WONG
JERRY HIKEN

3 GODS   1ST COSTUME
          ACT I

#1. HAL GOULD
#2. BILL SHARP
#3. BOB LOPEZ

3 GODS   2ND COSTUME
          SC 6A
          SC 7A

the audience from the real problems of the offstage revolt. The various levels of reality in this play are so complex that even the offstage revolt may be a trick, another theatrical improvisation that leaves only the black actors and the smokescreen of their diversions as concrete fact.

There is no real characterization in *The Blacks;* various stereotypes or ritualized images are merely donned by an actor at a particular moment, only to be put aside for another image at another moment. Characters are used only to create an image or to comment upon human experience within the shifting levels of the action. In his play, Genêt cut through the logical discussion and rational debates of the modern world to the darker recesses of the inner mind—to the level of myth, fear, masochistic fantasy, primitive ritual, and human sacrifice—and thus created a world of collective ecstasy and purgation, where man is forced to see all his values and realities as an endless progression and distortion of his own reflected thoughts and ideas. The language of such a drama is full of images that constantly try to shift the audience's perception of reality from one level to another. All the possible meanings and connotations of the word *black* are played off against the word *white* until the unconsciously held ideas of the audience are turned inside out and upside down. The rhythm of the play is like the visual movement of a kaleidoscope, rising and falling with the blending and pulling apart of the various levels of reality. There is no overall rhythm devised for the entire evening; each level of reality must seek its own rhythm.

The costumes should suggest both the primitive, ritual elements in the play and the blacks' satirical view of the power figures of the white establishment (Fig. 115). The costumes devised for the Queen, the Bishop, the Judge, the Governor-General, and the Valet should be an admixture of overdrawn caricaturing of white establishment figures and symbols that a white audience would associate with darkest Africa: grass trim, shells, carved jewelry, large bracelets and earrings, painted bodies, and animal-tooth ornaments. The velvet of the Queen's gown might turn abruptly to reeds, a sophisticated crown might sprout teeth, claws or

Figure 115
Costume sketches for *The Blacks* by Genêt, designed by Jean Schulz Davidson as a project, 1966. Note the intermingling of African and western European reality in the costumes. Courtesy Jean Schulz Davidson

Figure 116
The General from *The Blacks* by Genêt, produced
by the English Stage Company at The Royal Court
Theatre, London, 1966. An example of multiple
reality in costume created with the help of a mask.
Courtesy Sandra Lousada, Whitecross Studio, London

Figure 117
A scene from *The Blacks* by Genêt, produced by
the Akademie der Künste, Berlin, 1964, as part
of the Berliner Festwochen. An example of the
many layers of reality that must be suggested in
the play by the settings and costumes. Courtesy
Akademie der Künst. Photo by Heinz Köster

feathers, or the Governor-General's uniform might stop at the knees, where his lower legs turn into those of an ape—suggestions of how the white audience subconsciously sees the black man (Fig. 116).

It is difficult to come to a cohesive or logical plan for a production of a play with as many levels of reality as this one. All that is required for the staging of *The Blacks* is a large hall or room where a stage has been set up on which to reenact the ritual murder, and a range of ramps or seats behind on which the black actors playing whites can place themselves. In the planning of the platforms and ramps the designer must create constructions in space that are both primitive and sophisticated, handmade and machine tooled, organic yet modular. Set pieces and properties must be part primitive symbol and part polished product, and an item like the coffin must appear to be at the same time a box from backstage, a sinister and primitive handhewn container, and a highly finished mortuary product. Creating the suggestion of many different levels simultaneously is an immense challenge to the designer, who must keep the audience unnerved and guessing about the planes of reality by creating symbolic mixtures that will upset and violate their usual feelings and preconceptions (Fig. 117).

10

The New Theatre

In conclusion, a word should be said about the contemporary scene of playwriting and production—about the so-called New Theatre of the 1960s and 1970s that has turned its back on the intellectualism of the absurdists and the inner emotionalism of the psychological realists.

Theatre artists today have obviously grown weary of merely reflecting or commenting on a bourgeois society that they view as totally corrupt. They refuse to reaffirm the old values of unity, clarity, directness, simplicity, and completeness in a theatrical presentation; instead, they want to regain contact with man's elemental, organic nature—with the sacred mystery out of which theatre first developed—and are willing to use any and all vehicles for the projection of their invisible world. Theatre artists dedicated to the New Theatre seem unable to make ideas and images collide through words and are frequently accused of wanting to destroy everything admired in theatre during the past century, particularly the spoken word. There is, of course, some truth in this accusation: the spoken word today does not have the same value it once had in our society. We are living in an age of images, and we may have to go through a long period of image saturation before we can emerge with a new sense of language.

The prophet of the New Theatre was the French genius Antonin Artaud, who railed against the sterility of bourgeois theatre and described from the depths of his imagination and intuition a "theatre of cruelty," working like the plague, through intoxication, infection, and magic. He envisaged a theatre in which the play, the event itself, stood in place of the text. Artaud's ideas, carried forward in the Royal Shakespeare Company's productions of *Marat/Sade* and *A Midsummer Night's Dream,* under the direction of Peter Brook, have had a tremendous impact on contemporary playwriting and production (Fig. 118). In American works like *Hair, Tom Payne, Futz,* and *Godspell,* in the efforts that have come out of the workshops of the Polish visionary, Jerzy Grotowski, and in much of the experimental work going on in theatre centers like Prague, Paris, and Rome, this new theatre of image and action has taken a strong hold (Fig. 119). By making words secondary to communication through movement and gesture, and by channeling the modes of expression, actors can reserve all of their powers of concentration for the physical and visual expression of a dramatic action. Through the mere presence of the performer the invisible becomes visible. Masks, make-up, and other traditional theatrical properties and accessories are rejected in favor of silence, noise, a ritualistic use of repeated patterns, and the climactic effects of group action.

The followers of Artaud find the surprise element and surrealistic incongruity of absurdist drama as dead as the psychological drama of naturalism. They are groping toward a more violent, less rational, more extreme, less verbal, more dangerous theatre than the theatre of the immediate past. Once the great excitement of participation in the "New Theatre has worn thin, what then? The major question that leading critics and commentators are asking is, What follows the shock? Although they see the New Theatre as a necessary antidote to the immediate past, they also see the need for a return to language if the New Theatre is to last.

The Happening, an offshoot of the New Theatre developed in artistic circles after World War II, screamed "Wake up! Live! See and Feel!" to a

Figure 118
A scene from The American Conservatory Theatre's production of the Royal Shakespeare Company's *A Midsummer Night's Dream,* directed by Peter Brook, designed by Sally Jacobs. Courtesy Royal Shakespeare Company

The New Theatre

217

The New Theatre

218

deadened and desensitized industrial society. The impulsive, meaningless acts and exercises of the Happening have now become a part of theatrical performance, but the New Theatre will die quickly unless a clear purpose and meaning are given to the theatrical instincts, enthusiasms, and sensitivities unleashed by the shock and excitement created by this new kind of theatre. The theatre today has awakened a great and powerful sleeping hunger in us all, and designers, directors, actors, and playwrights are implicitly challenged to meet the need. Whether new forms with depth, perception, and meaning can be developed from the experiments of the New Theatre remains to be seen, but it is an exciting period of transition and change in which the best insights and instincts of all workers in the theatre may be shared and developed.

Figure 119
Eron Tabor (*center*) and the Tribe in a scene from the San Francisco production of *Hair,* presented by Michael Butler, Marshal Naify, and The American Conservatory Theatre. An example of the new theatre of image and action where verbal communication becomes subordinate to ritual communication through group action. Courtesy American Conservatory Theatre, San Francisco, California. Photo by Hank Kranzler

The New Theatre

Bibliography

General

Altman, George, et al. *Theatre Pictorial: A History of World Theatre as Recorded in Drawings, Paintings, Engravings and Photographs.* Berkeley and Los Angeles: University of California Press, 1953. A handy pictorial reference work on the development of theatre from earliest times to the middle of the twentieth century.

Brockett, Oscar. *The Theatre: An Introduction.* 3d ed. New York: Holt, Rinehart and Winston, 1974. A good introduction to all aspects of the theatre. The brief section on theatre history, with its select play analyses, is particularly good.

_____. *History of the Theatre.* 2d ed. Boston: Allyn and Bacon, 1974. A well-organized and complete general history of the theatre. The best book on the subject.

De la Croix, Horst, and Tansey, Richard G., eds. *Gardner's Art Through the Ages.* 6th ed. New York: Harcourt, Brace and World, 1975. An excellent and quite complete history of world art.

Gascoigne, Bamber. *World Theatre: An Illustrated History.* Boston: Little, Brown & Co., 1968. An excellent history of the theatre with unusual pictorial selections that cannot be found in other general histories of the theatre.

Gassner, John, and Allen, Ralph. *Theatre and Drama in the Making.* Boston: Houghton Mifflin Co., 1964. An excellent compendium of original source material on the history of the theatre, writing of plays, actors, critics, and performances.

Hartnoll, Phyllis. *Oxford Companion to the Theatre*. 3d ed. London: Oxford University Press, 1967. The best single reference volume available to the student of the theatre.

Hauser, Arnold. *The Social History of Art*. 4 vols. New York: Vintage Trade Books, Random House, 1959. An excellent history of the artistic and cultural development of Western man and the artist in Western culture from the early cave paintings to the middle of the twentieth century.

Janson, H. W. *History of Art*. Englewood Cliffs, N.J.: Prentice-Hall, 1969. Another excellent history of art that is very simply and clearly written to introduce the student to the mainstream of artistic development in the Western world.

Oenslager, Donald. *Scenery Then and Now*. New York: W. W. Norton & Co., 1936. A somewhat dated but charming book that introduces the student of design to the great periods of culture and demonstrates how designers included cultural aspects of a period in their approach to the staging of plays.

_____. *Stage Design: Four Centuries of Scenic Innovation*. New York: Viking Press, 1975. A beautifully designed book with pictorial material never before published on theatrical scenery since the beginning of the Renaissance.

Squire, Geoffrey. *Dress and Society, 1560–1970*. New York: Viking Press, 1974. An excellent study of the relationship between the visual arts and cultural ideals of a period and their involvement in the development of fashion.

Introduction

Fergusson, Francis. *The Idea of a Theatre: A Study of Ten Plays*. Princeton, N.J.: Princeton University Press, 1949. An excellent series of essays on key plays in the development of the drama, with special emphasis on how each play's structural composition reflects the cultural ideals of the period in which it was written.

Fry, Roger. *Vision and Design*. New York: Brentano's, 1924. A standard classic on the philosophy of man's ways of seeing and his sense of design.

Laver, James. *Style in Costume*. New York: Oxford University Press, 1949. An excellent book for helping the student of costume trace the nature of stylistic changes in fashion.

Rothschild, Lincoln. *Style in Art: The Dynamics of Art as Cultural Expression*. New York: Thomas Yoseloff Publisher, 1960. A very useful book for understanding the origins of style and the idea of the irrational versus the rational as the basis for stylistic change.

St. Denis, Michel. *The Rediscovery of Style*. New York: Theatre Arts Books, 1960. One of the best analyses of the nature of style in the theatre by one of the masters of the twentieth century stage.

Wölfflin, Heinrich. *Principles of Art History: The Problem of the Development of Style in Later Art.* New York: Dover Publications, 1950. Presents, through an examination of artistic polarities, the now classic contrast between the stylistic characteristics of the Renaissance and the Baroque. Wöfflin's basic principles for defining style can be applied to other important artistic periods.

_____. *The Sense of Form in Art: A Comparative Psychological Study.* New York: Chelsea Publishing Co., 1958. An interesting companion volume to *Principles of Art History* on the psychological responses of viewers to the form of an artistic work.

Chapter 1

Bieber, Margarete. *The History of the Greek and Roman Theatre.* 2d ed. Princeton, N.J.: Princeton University Press, 1961. The most comprehensive illustrated work in English on the nature of the classical theatre.

Brooke, Iris. *Costume in Greek Classic Drama.* New York: Theatre Arts Books, 1965. An excellent book, illustrated with line drawings, on the nature of Greek theatrical dress and how it was made.

Hamilton, Edith. *The Greek Way.* New York: W. W. Norton & Co., 1952. An excellent introduction to all aspects of Greek life and culture.

_____. *The Roman Way.* New York: W. W. Norton & Co., 1932. An excellent introduction to all aspects of Roman life and culture.

Harsh, Philip W. A. *Handbook of Classical Drama.* Stanford, Calif.: Stanford University Press, 1941. This is still a very useful reference book on classical drama.

Webster, T. B. L. *Greek Theatre Production.* New York: Barnes & Noble, 1956. A readable, comprehensive overview of Greek theatre and its production methods by one of the finest classical scholars of recent times.

Chapter 2

Kernodle, George. *From Art to Theatre.* Chicago: University of Chicago Press, 1944. One of the seminal books on the relationship between the visual arts and the theatre. Kernodle traces this relationship from early medieval through Renaissance times.

Nicoll, Allardyce. *Masks, Mimes and Miracles.* New York: Harcourt Brace Jovanovich, Inc., 1931. A slightly dated yet useful book on the nature of medieval play production.

Wickham, Glynne. *Early English Stages 1300–1660.* 2 vols. New York: Columbia University Press, 1959–1962. A superb and very detailed history of drama and play production in England during medieval times.

Williams, Arnold. *The Drama of Medieval England.* East Lansing: Michigan State University Press, 1961. A good summary of the structural elements of the various forms of medieval drama in England.

Chapter 3

Beckerman, Bernard. *Shakespeare at the Globe, 1599–1609.* New York: Macmillan Co., 1962. An excellent summary of the scholarship on the nature of theatrical productions at the Globe Theatre during the ten-year period in which Shakespeare wrote his major plays.

Burckhardt, Jakob C. *The Civilization of the Renaissance in Italy.* 3d ed. Vienna: Phaidon Art Books, 1937. The classic nineteenth century introductory work on the Renaissance by one of the most distinguished nineteenth century historians. Although Burckhardt's capitalist-mercantile outlook pervades the book, he brilliantly introduces the reader to the excitement of Renaissance culture.

Hodges, C. W. *The Globe Restored: A Study of the Elizabethan Theatre.* rev. ed. London: Oxford University Press, 1968. A beautiful author-illustrated book on the Globe stage and the surrounding theater by a man who has devoted his life to a study of the Globe.

Joseph, Bertram. *Elizabethan Acting.* 2d ed. London: Oxford University Press, 1964. An interesting theoretical analysis of acting during the Elizabethan era.

Kennard, Joseph S. *The Italian Theatre.* 2 vols. New York: William Edwin Rudge, 1932. The standard work on the nature of the Commedia dell' Arte.

Nicoll, Allardyce. *Stuart Masques and the Renaissance Stage.* New York: Harcourt Brace 1938. A highly regarded, excellently illustrated work that presents the development of court staging in Italy and its influence on the masque presentations at the court of England during the early seventeenth century.

Sypher, Wylie. *Four Stages of Renaissance Style: Transformations in Art and Literature.* Garden City, N.Y.: Doubleday-Anchor, 1955. Although written with a somewhat heavy hand, this is a brilliant work. It weaves together the stylistic characteristics at work in art and literature during the fifteenth, sixteenth, and seventeenth centuries.

Wölfflin, Heinrich. *Classic Art: An Introduction to the Italian Renaissance.* New York: Phaidon Art Books, 1952. The classic introduction to the artistic principles of the High Renaissance in Italy.

Chapter 4

Baur-Heinhold, M. *Baroque Theatre,* New York: McGraw-Hill Book Co., 1967. The finest pictorial compendium published to date on the theatre of the seventeenth and eighteenth centuries.

Hotson, John Leslie. *The Commonwealth and Restoration Stage.* Cambridge, Mass.: Harvard University Press, 1928. A standard summary of the theatrical developments in England during the second half of the seventeenth century.

Major, A. H. *The Bibiena Family.* New York: Bittner, 1945. The best known study on the history and methods of this famous Italian family of theatrical designers during the Baroque.

Odell, G. C. D. *Shakespeare from Betterton to Irving.* 2 vols. New York: Benjamin Blom, 1963. An excellent history of Shakespearean production in England during the seventeenth, eighteenth, and nineteenth centuries.

Turnell, Martin. *The Classical Moment: Studies in Corneille, Molière and Racine.* New York: New Directions Publishing, 1946. An excellent statement on the nature of the classical method of playwriting followed by the three masters of the drama in France during the late seventeenth century.

Wittkower, Rudolf. *Art and Architecture in Italy, 1600–1750.* Baltimore: Penguin Books, 1958. A scholarly treatment of Baroque art as it developed in Italy during the seventeenth and early eighteenth centuries.

Chapter 5

Boas, Frederick. *An Introduction to Eighteenth Century Drama, 1700–1780.* Oxford: Clarendon Press, 1953. A fine introductory work that has clear insight into the shift from tearful to high comedy during the eighteenth century.

Burnim, Kalman. *David Garrick, Director.* Pittsburgh, Pa.: Pittsburgh University Press, 1961. An excellent presentation of the directorial innovations of this famous eighteenth century English actor.

Hawkins, Frederick. *The French Stage in the Eighteenth Century.* 2 vols. 1888. Reprint. Westport, Conn.: Greenwood Press, 1969. An old but still useful book on the nature of French theatre during the age of Voltaire.

Kimball, Sidney Fiske. *The Creation of the Rococo.* Philadelphia, Pa.: Philadelphia Museum of Art, 1943. One of the best books, beautifully illustrated, on the development of this last aristocratic and elegant style before the triumph of bourgeois taste.

Scholz, Janos. *Baroque and Romantic Stage Design.* New York: E. P. Dutton & Co., 1962. A fine pictorial survey of the shift in outlook on the part of scenic designers from the seventeenth to the early nineteenth century.

Sypher, Wylie. *Rococo to Cubism in Art and Literature.* New York: Vintage Trade Books, Random House, 1963. This is heavy reading, but an excellent interweaving of the artistic and literary stylistic methods from the eighteenth through the early twentieth century.

Chapter 6

Delacroix, Eugéne. *The Journal of Eugéne Delacroix*. Translated and edited by Walter Pach. New York: Crown Publishers, 1948. The book affords brilliant insight into the attitudes and ideas of the most famous artist of the romantic movement in France.

Lucas, F. L. *The Decline and Fall of the Romantic Ideal*. Cambridge: At the University Press, 1936. An excellent study of the problems, particularly those of technique and structure, that confronted romantic artists.

Novotny, Fritz. *Painting and Sculpture in Europe, 1780–1880*. Baltimore: Penguin Books, 1960. One of the best statements on trends in art from before the French Revolution to just prior to the rise of Art Nouveau.

Rowell, George. *The Victorian Theatre*. Oxford: Clarendon Press, 1956. A unique insight into the atmosphere and artistic outlook on the English stage in the late nineteenth century.

Vardac, Nicholas. *Stage to Screen: Theatrical Method from Garrick to Griffith*. Cambridge, Mass.: Harvard University Press, 1949. An interesting book on the development of the realistic-romantic staging that culminated in the spectacle of the early films.

Chapter 7

Gorelik, Mordecai. *New Theatres for Old*. New York: E. P. Dutton & Co., 1962. A brilliant study of the stylistic changes in theatre from realism through Brechtian relativism.

Melcher, Edith. *Stage Realism in France from Diderot to Antoine*. Bryn Mawr, Pa.: Bryn Mawr Press, 1928. A scholarly presentation of realism in French theatre and drama.

Nicoll, Allardyce. "History of Late Nineteenth Century Drama." In *A History of English Drama, 1660–1900*. vol. 5. Cambridge: At the University Press, 1930. A very useful standard history of the period in which realism developed in England.

Sloane, Joseph C. *French Painting Between the Past and Present: Artists, Critics, and Traditions from 1840 through 1870*. Princeton, N.J.: Princeton University Press, 1951. A concentrated study of painting in France at the moment of the triumph of realism.

Waxman, S. M. *Antoine and the Théâtre-Libre*. Cambridge, Mass.: Harvard University Press, 1926. A study of the contributions to realism of this most famous of innovators in stage realism.

Chapter 8

Appia, Adolphe. *The Work of Living Art: A Theory of the Theatre*. Coral Gables, Florida: University of Miami Press, 1960. Gives an excellent idea of the theories of impressionistic symbolism (the "New Stagecraft") in staging with particular emphasis on the importance of lighting in capturing dramatic mood.

Bergson, Henri. *The Creative Mind.* Translated by Mabelle L. Andison. New York: Philosophical Library, 1946. An important philosophical work that explains the impressionistic-symbolist interest in changing moods and the passing moment.

Craig, Edward Gordon. *On the Art of the Theatre.* New York: Theatre Arts Books, 1957. The best book for understanding this designer-theorist's demand for a single, aesthetic, artistic control in the theatre and his stress on theatrical mood and simplicity.

Jones, Robert Edmond. *The Dramatic Imagination.* New York: Theatre Arts Books, 1941. An inspiring and stimulating book on theatrical design by the leading symbolist designer in America in the early twentieth century.

Lehmann, Andrew G. *The Symbolist Aesthetic in France, 1885–1895.* 2d ed. New York: Barnes & Noble, 1968. An excellent overview of the symbolist movement during its major period of impact.

Stein, Jack M. *Richard Wagner and the Synthesis of the Arts.* Detroit, Michigan: Wayne State University Press, 1960. A good introduction to the development of symbolism. Stein stresses the importance of Wagner as a key figure in synthesizing the visual, verbal, and musical arts and in stressing the idea of mood and subliminal ideas in musical dramas.

Chapter 9

Artaud, Antonin. *The Theater and Its Double.* Translated by Mary C. Richards. New York: Grove Press, 1959. Artaud, one of the most influential theatrical theorists of the twentieth century, develops his theory of the "theatre of cruelty" and physical-emotional response to dramatic action.

Brustein, Robert. *The Theatre of Revolt: An Approach to the Modern Drama.* Boston: Little, Brown & Co., 1964. This book gives a succinct overview of the antiestablishment theatre of the fifties and early sixties.

Esslin, Martin. *The Theatre of the Absurd.* Garden City, N. Y.: Doubleday & Company, 1969. An important book of the mid-twentieth century that characterizes and labels the playwrights of the absurd and defines their views of reality.

Haftmann, Werner. *Painting in the Twentieth Century.* rev ed. Translated by Ralph Manheim. 2 vols. New York: Praeger Publishers, 1965. A very important work on the development of modern painting from the fauvists and early expressionists, through the action painters, to the early op and pop artists.

Hainaux, René, ed. *Stage Design Throughout the World Since 1935.* New York: Theatre Arts Books, 1956. An impressive visual coverage in designs and photographs in color and black and white of costume and stage design in all the leading countries of the world from 1935 to 1950.

_____. *Stage Design Throughout the World Since 1950.* New York: Theatre Arts Books, 1964. A companion volume to *Stage Design Throughout the World Since 1935* that brings the pictorial record up to date through the early 1960s.

Southern, Richard. *The Open Stage.* New York: Theatre Arts Books, 1959. A helpful study of the redevelopment in the twentieth century of the various forms of the thrust and open stages in which audiences surround much of the acting area.

Chapter 10

Brook, Peter. *Empty Space: A Book About the Theatre: Deadly, Holy, Rough, Immediate.* New York: Atheneum Publishers, 1968. An important book dealing with the four kinds of theatre that Brook saw around him in the late sixties: the deadly, the holy, the rough, and the immediate theatres. Many of Brook's ideas stem from the theories of Antonin Artaud.

Langer, Susanne. *Problems of Art: Ten Philosophical Lectures.* New York: Charles Scribner's Sons, 1957. An important twentieth century theory of visual aesthetics.

Richman, Robert, ed. *The Arts at Mid-Century.* New York: Horizon Press, 1954. A helpful summary of what was accomplished in the arts during the first half of the twentieth century.

Smith, C. Ray, ed. *The Theatre Crafts Book of Costume.* Emmaus, Pa.: Rodale Press, 1973. A collection of articles on costume from *Theatre Crafts Magazine* from 1967 through 1972, including an article by this author on the 1966 Stanford Repertory Theatre production of Aeschylus' *Prometheus Bound.*

Index

Titles of plays are printed in *italics,* titles of works of art in SMALL CAPITALS. References to illustrations are printed in **boldface** type.

Abbey Theatre, Dublin, 150
Abstractionism, 20, 21, 147, 190, 194, 196
Absurdism, 199
Actor Prepares, An (Stanislavsky; book), 153
Actor training, Russian systems of, 153, 196
Adams, Henry, *Mont St. Michel and Chartres* (book), 51
Aeschylus, 35, 37. See also *Prometheus Bound*
Akademie der Kunste, production by, **213**
Alexander, George, **137**
Alexander VI (pope), 67
Altamira cave, Paleolithic painting in, **19**
American Conservatory Theatre, productions by, **5, 41, 74, 113, 164, 201, 217–18**

Anderson, Mary, **81**
ANNUNCIATION TO THE SHEPHERED (from Sacramentary of Fulda), **54**
Antoine, André, 150
Antony and Cleopatra (Shakespeare), 70
ANTWERP ADORATION, THE (Rubens), **9**
APA-Phoenix Repertory Company, production by, **165**
Apollo, 32
APOLLO AND DAPHNE (Bernini), **92**
Appia, Adolphe, 3, 170, 173
    DESIGN FOR PARSIFAL, **174**
Aquinas, Thomas, 51
Aristophanes, 37, 39
    Birds, The, 37
    Clouds, The, 37
    Frogs, The, 37
    Knights, The, 37
    Lysistrata, 37, 39

Aristotle, 99
Art nouveau, 168
Artaud, Antonin, 216
AUTUMN RHYTHM (Pollock), **195**

Ball, William, productions directed by, **5, 41, 74, 164**
BALZAC (Rodin), **6**
Baptistry in Florence, Ghiberti's door panels for, 8, **8**
Baroque architecture, 8, 13, **13**
Baroque art, 75
    classical, 93, **94,** 95, 97
    operatic, 93, 97
    realism in, 95, **96**
Baroque comedy. *See* Molière; Restoration comedy
Baroque costumes, 97, **98**
Baroque opera, 10, 97
Baroque theaters, 95, 97
Basonge tribal mask, **28**

Baudelaire, Charles Pierre, 167
Bayreuth, Wagner's theater at, 170
Beaumarchais, Pierre de, 122
Belasco, David, 4
Bel Geddes, Norman. *See* Geddes,
   Norman Bel
Belgian National Theatre, production
   by, **182**
Bellelli Family, The (Degas),
   158, **159**
Bernini, Gian Lorenzo, 93
   Apollo and Daphne, **92**
Biblical stories, dramatization of, 52,
   55, 56, 57, 58. See also
   The Second Shepherd's Play
Biomechanics, 196
Birds, The (Aristophanes), 37
Blackman, Bob, settings by, **164**
Blacks, The (Genêt), 4
   analysis of, 208, 211
   costumes for, **210**, 211,
        212–13, 214
   scenery and settings for, **213**, 214
Blenheim Palace (Vanbrugh), 111
Borromini, Francesco (Church of
   San Carlo alle Quattro
   Fontane), 13, **13**
Botticelli, Sandro, 6, 15, 17, 79, 82
   Adoration of the Kings, The, **78**
   Judith with the Head of
        Holofernes, **7**
Bowers, Mrs. D. P., **2**
Bramante, Donato, 67
   Tempietto, San Pietro in
        Montorio, Rome, **12**, 13
Braque, Georges, 190
Brecht, Berthold, 196, 199, 203, 204,
   205. See also *The Goodwoman
   of Setzuan*
Brieux, Eugène, 150
Brook, Peter, production directed
   by, 216, **217**
Brunelleschi, Filippo, 67

Burgtheater, Vienna, 131, 140
Burial of Count Orgaz, The
   (El Greco), **84**, 86
Bury, John, design by, **90**
Butler, Michael, presentation by, **218**
Byron, George Gordon, Lord, 133

Callot, Jacques, sketches of Italian
   comedy figures by, **72**, 73
Caravaggio, Michelangelo da, 95
Carnival of Harlequin (Miró), **17**
Carracci, Agostino, 93
Carracci, Annibale, 93
Cathedrals. *See* Gothic cathedrals
Catholic Church, scope given
   Renaissance artists by, 67
Cave paintings, 18, **19**
Cervantes, Miguel de, 65
Cézanne, Paul, 190
   Mont Sainte Victoire, **192**
Charles II (king of England), 107–8
Chartres Cathedral, royal portal of,
   62, 64
Chekhov, Anton, 153, 161, 162, 163,
   189. See also *The Cherry
   Orchard*
Cherry Orchard, The (Chekhov),
   152, **164–65**, 165
   analysis of, 161–62
   costumes for, 163, **164–65**, 165
   lighting for, 163
   settings for, 162–63, **164**
Chorus, Greek, 32, 39
Christ and the Pilgrims of Emmaus
   (Velásquez), **96**
Church plays, 52, 55, **56–57**, 58
Cibber, Colley, *Love's Last Shift*, 111
Circus Schumann, Berlin, 196
Clairon, Mlle (Claire-Josèphe Léris),
   120
Clark, Henry, production directed
   by, **63**

Classicism, 13
   defined, 18
   Baroque, 93, 95
   of Cézanne, 190, **192**
   18th century, 116, **118**
Clouds, The (Aristophanes), 37
Collage, 194, 200, 203
Comaro, Alexander, costumes
   by, **141**
Comédie Française, 120, 131
Comedy
   18th century, 122 (see also
        The School for Scandal)
   Elizabethan comedy, 122
   French (*see* Molière)
   Greek, 37, 39, 45, 50
   Italian, **72**, 73, 104
   Renaissance, 10, 73
   Restoration, 96, 107, 108 (see
        also *The Relapse*)
   Roman, 47, **48–49**, 49, 50, 73, 104
   Shakespearean, 74
   See also Commedia dell'arte
Commedia dell'arte, **72**, 73, **74**,
   95, 104
Composition (Mondrian), **16**
Comte, Auguste, 145
Constructivism, 196
Copeau, Jacques, basic architectural
   stage by, 196, **197**
Copernicus, Nicolaus, 91
Costumes, 15
   ambiguities in, **2**, 3, **81**, 134, **136**
   Baroque, 97, **98**
   for *Blacks, The*, **210**, 211,
        212–13, 214
   for *Cherry Orchard, The*, 163, **164**,
        165, **165**
   in 18th century productions, 120,
        124, 125
   Elizabethan, **2**, 4, 77, **77**, **81**
   for *Faust*, **137**, 140, 143
   for *From Morn to Midnight*, 186, 188

for *Ghosts*, **156**, 158, 161
for *Goodwoman of Setzuan, The*,
    208, **209**
Greek, **26**, 27, **30**, 32, 134, **136**
for *Hamlet*, 86, 88, **89**
historical accuracy of, 120, 123,
    133, 134, **135, 137**
for medieval plays, 55, 58, 64
for *Menaechmi*, 47, **48**, 50
in 19th century productions, 133,
    134, **135–36**, 137
for *Oedipus Rex*, 40, 43, 45
for *Pelléas et Mélisande*, 180, **182**,
    183–84
for *Phèdre*, 100, **101–2**, 103
for *Prometheus Bound*, 25, **26**, 27
for *Relapse, The*, 112
for *Romeo and Juliet*, **81**, 82
for *School for Scandal, The*, 123,
    124, 125, 127
for *Second Shepherd's Play, The*,
    60, 64
for *Six Characters in Search of an
    Author*, 203
for *Tartuffe*, **5**, 105, 107
Courbet, Gustave, 149
    Funeral at Ornans, The, **149**
    Stonebreakers, The, 149
Covent Garden, London, 133
Craig, Gordon, 3, 173
    sketch for ideal theatre by, **175**
Crommelynck, Fernand, *The
    Magnificent Cuckold*, **198**
Cubism
    in art, 190, 194
    in theatre, 194, 196, 199–200

Danchenko, Vladimir. *See*
    Nemirovich-Danchenko,
    Vladimir
Dante Alighieri, 51, 178
Dante and Virgil in Hell
    (Delacroix), **128**

Darwin, Charles, theories of,
    147, 189
David (Donatello), **66**
David, Jacques Louis, 116
    The Lictors Bringing to Brutus
        the Bodies of His Sons, **118**
David (Michelangelo), 6, **68**
Davidson, Jean Schulz, costumes
    by, **210**
Da Vinci. *See* Leonardo da Vinci
Day of the God, The (Gauguin),
    170, **171**
Debussy, Claude, 168
    Pelléas et Mélisande (opera), 168,
        178, **179**, 180, **181**, 183
Degas, Edgar, 147, 163
    Bellelli Family, The, 158, **159**
    Interior: The Rape, or The
        Seduction, 158, **160**
Delacroix, Eugène, 129, 189
    Dante and Virgil in Hell, **128**
    Faust in His Study, **142**, 143
De Mille, Cecil B., 4
Denial of St. Peter, The
    (Rembrandt), **7**
Design for Parsifal (Appia), **174**
Designer
    as interpreter, 21–22
    preparatory work of, 4, 6, 20–22
De Witt, Johann, sketch of Swan
    Theatre by, 76
Diderot, Denis, 116
Dionysiac festivals, 31
Dionysus, 31, 32
Director, interpretative options of,
    21, 22
Donatello, 67
    David, **66**
Double-cubed Room, Wilton House
    (Webb), **109**
Double reality, 196
Dream, The, or Reverie (Redon),
    168, **169**

Drury Lane Theatre, London, 133
    performance at, 123, **124**
    interior of, **132**
Dryden, John, 91
Dying Gaul, The, **38**
Dying Niobid, The, **36**

Eakins, Thomas, 147
    The Pathetic Song, **146**
1814 (Meissonier), **148**, 149
El Greco. *See* Greco, El
Elizabeth I (queen of England),
    play based on life of, **2**, 3
Elizabethan costumes, **2**, 4, 77,
    77, 81
Elizabethan plays, 75, 77, **77**, 79
    196. *See also* Shakespeare
Elizabethan stage and theater, 70, 75,
    76, 77, 80, 85
    return to concept of, 194, 196
Elizabethan Stage Society, 194, 196
England, 83, 115
    as cultural crossroads, 73, 75
    mannerism during Renaissance
        in, 73, 83
English Stage Company, production
    by, **212**
Ensor, James, 170
Epic theatre, 196, 199, **207**
Essex Rebellion, 82
Euripides, 37
    Hippolytus, 99
Everyman (morality play), 58
Expressionism, 20, 168
    abstract, 194, **195**
    in art, 131, 170, 194, **195**
    in theatre, 170, 177, 184, 186, 188
        (see also *From Morn to
        Midnight*)

Farces, medieval secular, 58
Faust (Goethe), 134, 137
    analysis of, 137–39

Index

Faust (*continued*)
  costumes for, **137**, 140, 143
  methods of staging, 139–40, **141**
FAUST IN HIS STUDY (Delacroix),
    142, 143
Fergusson, Francis, 147
Festival of Corpus Christi, 55
Flaubert, Gustave, 147
Fletcher, Robert, designs by, **41**, **74**
Fort, Paul, 170
Four Stages of Renaissance Style
    (Sypher; book), 15
France, Baroque art in, 93, 95
Freie Bühne, Berlin, 150
French Academy, 93
French comedy. *See* Molière
French Revolution, 129
Friedrich, Caspar David, 88
  MAN AND WIFE GAZING AT THE
    MOON, **87**
Frogs, The (Aristophanes), 37
From Morn to Midnight (Kaiser), **187**
  analysis of, 184–85
  costumes for, 186, 188
  settings and lighting for, 186
*From Rococo to Cubism in Art and
    Literature* (Sypher; book), 199
FUNERAL AT ORNANS, THE
    (Courbet), **149**
Futz, 216

Gainsborough, Thomas, 127
  MRS. GRAHAM, **126**
Galileo, 91
Garrick, David, 120
GATES OF HELL, THE (Rodin), **191**
Gauguin, Paul, THE DAY OF THE GOD,
    170, **171**
Geddes, Norman Bel, 173
Genêt, Jean, 208. See also *The Blacks*
George II, Duke of Saxe-Meiningen,
    150

Ghiberti, Lorenzo, 8, 79
  SOLOMON RECEIVING THE QUEEN OF
    SHEBA, **8**
Ghosts (Ibsen), 161, 165
  analysis of, 153–54, 157, 162
  costumes for, **156**, 158, 161
  scenery and settings for, **155–56,**
    157–58
Giotto, 60, 67, 194
  MEETING OF JOACHIM AND
    ANNA, **61**
Gissey, Henri, costume by, **98**
Godspell, 216
Goethe, Johann Wolfgang von, 137,
    138, 139, 143. See also *Faust*
Gogh, Vincent van, 131, 170, 189
Goldoni, Carlo, 122
Goldsmith, Oliver, 122
Goodwoman of Setzuan, The
    (Brecht), **207**
  analysis of, 203–5
  costumes for, 208, **209**
  scenery and settings for, 205
Gothic art, 52, **54**, 60, **61–62,** 64.
  See also Gothic cathedrals
Gothic cathedrals, 51–52, **53**, 55,
    62, 64
Gothic literature, 52
Gozzoli, Benozzo, THE JOURNEY OF
    THE MAGI, **14**, 15
Greco, El, 69, 83, 88
  BURIAL OF COUNT ORGAZ, THE,
    84, 86
  VIEW OF TOLEDO, 10, **11,** 15
Greek architecture, **31**
Greek chorus, 32, 39
Greek comedy, 37, 39, 45, 50
Greek costumes, **26**, 27, **30**, 32,
    134, **136**
Greek masks, **26**, 27, 31, 32, 35
Greek sculpture, **34**, **36**, **38**, 45
Greek theaters, 32, **33**

Greek tragedy, 31–32, 35, 37
  as source for *Phèdre*, 99, 100
  See also *Oedipus Rex*
Greenwood, Jane, costumes by, **5**
Greuze, Jean Baptiste, 116
  THE RETURN OF THE PRODIGAL, **117**
Grosses Schauspielhaus, Berlin, 196
Grotowski, Jerzy, 216
Guthrie Theater, The, **35**, **44**

Hagen, Uta, **165**
Hair, 216, **218**
Hall, Peter, production directed
    by, **90**
Hamlet (Shakespeare), 4, 8, 82, 88,
    90
  analysis of, 83, 85
  costumes for, 86, 88, **89**
  lighting for, 86
  scenery and settings for,
    85–86, 88
Happening, 216, 219
Headdresses, 29
Heilinger, Bernhard, scenery by, **141**
Henry IV (Shakespeare), 73
Henslowe, Philip, 77
Herbert, Jocelyn, designs by, **156**
Hin und Zurück (Hindemith;
    opera), **23**
Hindemith, Paul, *There and Back
    (Hin und Zurück)* (opera), **23**
Hippolytus (Euripides), 99
Historical accuracy, 21
  in 18th century productions, 120
  in 19th century productions,
    133–34, **135**, 137, 150
  pitfalls of, 3–4
Hogarth, William, 116
HOLY FAMILY ON THE STEPS
    (Poussin), **94**
Hoover (Lou Henry) Pavilion,
    Stanford University, **24**

Index

Hopkins, Arthur, production directed and produced by, **177**
Hugo, Victor, 133
Humanism, 52, 65

Ibsen, Henrik, 147, 150, 153, 154, 161, 163, 189. See also *Ghosts*
Impressionism, 20, 168
  in art, 163, 168, **169**, 170, 189, 190, **192**
  in music, 168
  in theatre, 165, **165**, 178, **179**, **181–82**, 183, 184 (see also *Pelléas et Mélisande*)
Independent Theatre, London, 150
Industrial Revolution, 145
INTERIOR: THE RAPE, or THE SEDUCTION (Degas), 158, **160**
INTERNAL AND EXTERNAL FORMS (Moore), **193**
International Gothic style, 60, 65
Irving, Henry, production by, **137**
"Isms," 18
Italy
  Baroque art in, 93
  Renaissance art in, 67
  Renaissance theatre in, 70
    commedia dell'arte, **72**, 73, **74**, 95, 104

Jacobs, Sally, designs by, **217**
Jones, Inigo, 108
Jones, Robert Edmond, 173
  designs by, **177**, **180**
JOURNEY OF THE MAGI, THE (Gozzoli), **14**, 15
JUDITH WITH THE HEAD OF HOLOFERNES (Botticelli), **7**
Julius Caesar (Shakespeare), 70, **151**
Julius II (pope), 67
Junk art, 205

Kaiser, Georg, 184, 185. See also *From Morn to Midnight*
Kean, Charles, 134, **135**
Kean, Mrs. Charles (Ellen), 134, **136**
Kemble, John Philip, 120
Kepler, Johannes, 91
Knights, The (Aristophanes), 37

LADY AND GENTLEMAN AT THE VIRGINALS, A (Vermeer), **106**
Langham, Michael, production directed by, **35**
Lapp art, **19**
LAST SUPPER, THE (Leonardo da Vinci), 10, **10**
LAST SUPPER, THE (Tintoretto), **69**, 86
Lekain, Henri Louis, 120
Lely, Peter, 108, 112
  TWO LADIES OF THE LAKE FAMILY, **110**
Leo X (pope), 67
Leonardo da Vinci, 65, 67
  LAST SUPPER, THE, 10, **10**
Lessing, Gotthold, 116
LICTORS BRINGING TO BRUTUS THE BODIES OF HIS SONS, THE (David), **118**
Lighting
  Appia's use of, 173, **174**
  in Baroque theaters, 95
  for *Cherry Orchard, The*, 163, **164**
  Craig's use of, **175**
  in 18th century productions, 120
  for Elizabethan stage, 77
  in expressionist dramas, 186
  for *Faust*, 139–40
  for *From Morn to Midnight*, 186
  for *Hamlet*, 86
  for *Pelléas et Mélisande*, **179**, 180, **181**, 183
  for *Phèdre*, 100

for *Six Characters in Search of an Author*, 203
for *Tartuffe*, 105
London, 123
Lou Henry Hoover Pavilion, Stanford University, **24**
Louis XV (king of France), 115
Louis XIV (king of France), 95, 108
Love's Last Shift (Cibber), 111
Lugne-Poë, Aurélien-Marie, 170
Lysistrata (Aristophanes), 37, 39

Macbeth (Shakespeare), 15, 138, **177**
Macklin, Charles, 120
Maeterlinck, Maurice, 168, 190. See also *Pelléas et Mélisande*
Magnificent Cuckold, The (Crommelynck), **198**
MAN AND WIFE GAZING AT THE MOON (Friedrich), **87**
Mannerism
  in art, 67, **69**, 70, **84**
  defined, 20
  in England during Renaissance, 73, 83
  in theatre, 25, 82
Marat/Sade (Weiss), 216
Masaccio, 67
Masks
  Basonge tribal, **28**
  for *Blacks, The*, **212**
  Greek, **26**, 27, 31, 32, 35
  as key visual accessory, 29, 31, 32, 35
  for *Menaechmi*, 50
  for *Oedipus Rex*, 40, 43
Master Pierre Pathelin (medieval farce), 58
Measure for Measure (Shakespeare), 15
MEETING OF JOACHIM AND ANNA (Giotto), **61**

Meissonier, Jean Louis Ernest, 1814, **148,** 149
Menaechmi (Plautus)
    analysis of, 47
    costumes for, 47, **48,** 50
    sets for, 47, 50
Mertz, Franz, stage model by, **42**
Merz Construction (Schwitters), **206**
Metamorphoses (Ovid; narrative poem), 93
Meyerhold, Vsevolod, production by, **198**
Michelangelo, 65, 67, 190
    David, 6, **68**
Midsummer Night's Dream, A (Shakespeare), 216, **217**
Mielziner, Jo, 173
Miracle, The, **176**
Miracle plays, 58
Miró, Joan, 15
    Carnival of Harlequin, **17**
Misanthrope, The (Molière), 6
Mrs. Graham (Gainsborough), **126**
Moffatt, Donald, **165**
Molière, 95, 107, 108
    comedies of, 97, 103, 104–5, 107, 108, 122
    Misanthrope, The, 6
    See also *Tartuffe*
Mondrian, Piet, 15, 194
    Composition, **16**
Monet, Claude, 163, 168
    Rouen Cathedral, **166**
Mont Sainte Victoire (Cézanne), **192**
Mont St. Michel and Chartres (Adams; book), 51
Moore, Henry, Internal and External Forms, **193**
Morality plays, 58
Moralizing, in 18th century theatre and art, 115, 116, **117,** 122, 123

Moscow Art Theatre, **152,** 153, 162
Multiple reality
    in art, 190, **193, 206**
    in theatre, 194, 196, 200, **201,** 203, 208, 210, **210,** **212–13,** 214
Munch, Edvard, 170, 189
    The Scream, **172**
Music, impressionistic, 168
Musical comedy, Roman, 47
My Life in Art (Stanislavsky; book), 153
Mystery plays, 55, 58, 60, **63.** See also *The Second Shepherd's Play*

Naify, Marshal, presentation by, **218**
Napoleon's Retreat from Moscow, or 1814 (Meissonier), **148,** 149
National Theatre of Oslo, production by, **155**
Naturalism, 19, 20, 45, **46,** 65, 116
Nemirovich-Danchenko, Vladimir, 153
Neolithic art, 18, **19**
Neomannerism, 168, 170, **171**
Neoplasticism, **16,** 194
New Comedy, Greek, 39, 45, 50
New Theatre, **217–18**
    development of, 215–16, 219
    outlook for, 216, 219
Notre Dame Cathedral, Paris, **52**

Oedipus Rex (Sophocles), 35, **35,** **41, 44**
    analysis of, 39–40, 83, 154
    costumes for, 40, 43, 45
    sets for, **42,** 43, 45
Oenslager, Donald, 173

Old Comedy, Greek, 37, 39
Op art, 194
Opera
    Baroque, 10, 93, 97
    comic, **23**
    impressionistic symbolism in, 168, 178, 180, **181,** 183
Orchestra, Greek, 32, 196
Othello (Shakespeare), 138
Ovid, *Metamorphoses* (narrative poem), 93

Paleolithic art, 18, **19**
Palladio, Andrea, theatre design by, 70, **71**
Paris, 216
Parthenon (Athens), model of, **31**
Passion play at Valenciennes, **56–57**
Pathetic Song, The (Eakins), **146**
Pelléas et Mélisande (Maeterlinck), 168, 170
    analysis of, 178, 180
    costumes for, 180, **182,** 183–84
    as opera (Debussy), 168, 178, **179,** 180, **181,** 183
    scenery and settings for, 180, 183
    as opera, **179, 181**
Perception, modes of. *See* Polarities
Phèdre (Racine)
    analysis of, 97, 99–100
    costumes for, 100, **101–2,** 103
    settings for, 100
Phylakes comedies, 49, **49**
Picasso, Pablo, 190
Pirandello, Luigi, 189, 199–200, 203. See also *Six Characters in Search of an Author*
Piscator, Erwin, 196
Plaisirs du Bal, Les (Watteau), **114**
Plautus, 45. See also *Menaechmi*
Poel, William, 196

Index

Polarities
    in art and theatre, 6, 8, 10,
        13–15, 17–18
    examples of, in art, **7, 8–10,**
        11–12, 13–14, 16–17, 19
Pollock, Jackson, 194
    Autumn Rhythm, **195**
Pont du Gard, The (Robert), **119**
Pop art, 194
Portrait of a Roman, **46**
Poseidon of Cape Artemision, 32,
    34, 35
Positivism, 145, 146
Poussin, Nicolas, 15, 93, 97, 100,
    103, 116
    The Holy Family, **94**
Prague, 216
Principles of Art History (Wölfflin;
    book), 6
Prometheus Bound (Aeschylus)
    costumes for, 25, **26**, 27, **30**
    scenery for, 25
    stress on visual aspects in, 31
Pugin and Rowlandson, illustration
    by, **132**
Pyne, Natasha, **156**

Racine, Jean, 6, 15, 91, 95, 97, 99,
    103. See also *Phèdre*
Rain, Steam and Speed
    (Turner), **130**
Raphael, 65, 67
    School of Athens, The, 15
Realism, 20, 145, 147
    in art, 95, **96**, 146, 147, **148–49,**
        149, 158, **159–60,** 167
    in theatre, 147, 150, **151–52,** 153,
        155–56, 164–65, 165, 199
    (see also *The Cherry*

Orchard; Ghosts)
    See also Historical accuracy
Redon, Odilon, 168
    Dream, The, or Reverie, 168, **169**
    Silence, 168
    Thought, The, 168
Reinhardt, Max, 173, 196
    production by, **176**
Relapse, The (Vanbrugh), **113**
    analysis of, 111
    costumes for, 112
    settings for, 112
Relativist concepts
    in art, 190, **193,** 194, **195**
    in theatre, 194, 196, **198,** 199
    (see also *The Blacks; The*
        Goodwoman of Setzuan; Six
        Characters in Search of an
        Author)
Rembrandt, 6, 15, 95
    Denial of St. Peter, The, **7**
Renaissance, 82
    architecture of, 8, **12,** 13
    art of, 65, **66,** 67, **68,** 69
    comedies of, 10
    English theatre during (*see*
        Elizabethan plays;
        Shakespeare)
    Italian theatre during, 70,
        71–72, 73
    three artistic periods of, 65, 67, 70
Renoir, Pierre Auguste, 163
Restoration comedy, 107, 108, 122.
    See also *The Relapse*
Restoration culture, 108
Return of the Prodigal, The
    (Greuze), **117**
Reverie, or The Dream (Redon),
    168, **169**
Richard II (Shakespeare), **135**
Richardson, Samuel, 116
Richardson-Romanesque architec-
    tural style, 22, **24**

Robbe-Grillet, Alain, 194
Robert, Hubert, 116
    The Pont du Gard, **119**
Rococo style, 115–16
Rodin, 190
    Balzac, 6
    Gates of Hell, The, **191**
Roman comedy, 47, **48–49,** 49, 50,
    73, 104. See also *Menaechmi*
Roman sculpture, 45, **46**
Roman theaters, 45–46, 70
Romanticism, 13, 116, 145, 167
    in art, **87, 119, 128,** 129, **130,**
        131, **142**
    defined, 18
    as fully conscious style, 129, 131
    in theatre, 82, 133, 137, **137,** 150
    (see also *Faust*)
Rome, 67, 216
Romeo and Juliet (Shakespeare), 8,
    15, **81**
    analysis of, 79–80
    costumes for, **81,** 82
    scenery and settings for, 80, 82
Rose, Clifford, **156**
Roth, Ann, costumes by, **164**
Rouen Cathedral (Monet), **166**
Rousseau, Jean Jacques, 116
Rowlandson. *See* Pugin and
    Rowlandson
Royal Shakespeare Company,
    productions by, **90, 156,**
    216, **217**
Royal Theater, Drottningholm,
    120, **121**
Rubens, Peter Paul, 8, 15, 93, 129
    The Antwerp Adoration, **9**
Russell, Douglas A., costumes by,
    48, 89, 101–2
Russian theatre
    actor training in, 153, 196
    constructivism in, 196
Ruta, Ken, **41**

Index

San Carlo alle Quattro Fontane, Church of (Borromini), 13, **13**
Sardou, Victorien, 153
Saxe-Meiningen, Duke of. *See* George II
Saxe-Meiningen Court Company, **151**
Scamozzi, Vincenzo, theatre design by, **71**
Scenery and settings, 15
  for *Blacks, The,* **213,** 214
  in 18th century productions, 120, **121, 124, 125**
  on Elizabethan stage, 70, 75, 77
  for *Faust,* 139–40, **141**
  for *From Morn to Midnight,* 186
  for *Ghosts,* **155–56,** 157–58
  for *Goodwoman of Setzuan, The,* 205
  in Greek tragedy, 32
  for *Hamlet,* 85–86, 88
  historical accuracy of, 123, 133
  in medieval plays, 55, 196
  for *Menaechmi,* 47, 50
  in mystery plays, 55
  in 19th century productions, 133–34, 150
  for *Oedipus Rex,* **42,** 43, 45
  for *Pelléas et Mélisande* (play), 180, 183; (opera), **179, 181**
  for *Phèdre,* 100
  for *Prometheus Bound,* 25
  for *Relapse, The,* 112
  in Roman theaters, 45
  for *Romeo and Juliet,* 80, 82
  for *School for Scandal, The,* 123, **124,** 125
  for *Second Shepherd's Play, The,* 59–60, 64
  for *Six Characters in Search of an Author,* 200, **201**
  symbolists' precepts and ideals re, 170, 173, **174–75**
  for *Tartuffe,* **5,** 105, 107

Schiller Theater (West Berlin), production by, 140, **141**
School for Scandal, The (Sheridan) analysis of, 122–23
  costumes for, 123, **124, 125,** 127
  sets for, 123, **124,** 125
Sᴄʜᴏᴏʟ ᴏꜰ Aᴛʜᴇɴs, Tʜᴇ (Raphael), 15
Schröder, Ernst, production directed by, **141**
Schwitters, Kurt, *Merz* constructions of, 205, **206**
Science, response of artists to, 145, 147, 149, 189–90
Sᴄʀᴇᴀᴍ, Tʜᴇ (Munch), **172**
Scribe, Eugène, 153
Second Shepherd's Play, The (mystery play), **63**
  analysis of, 58–60
  costumes for, 60, 64
  scenery and settings for, 59–60, 64
Sᴇᴅᴜᴄᴛɪᴏɴ, Tʜᴇ, ᴏʀ Iɴᴛᴇʀɪᴏʀ: Tʜᴇ Rᴀᴘᴇ (Degas), 158, 160
Sentimentality, 18th century
  in art, **114,** 115, 116, **117,** 120
  in theatre, 120, 122, 123
Settings. *See* Scenery and settings
Shakespeare, William, 6, 15, 65, 75, 120, 137, 138
  Antony and Cleopatra, 70
  development pattern of works of, 75
  Henry IV, 73
  influence of Italian theatre on, 70, 73
  Julius Caesar, 70, **151**
  Macbeth, 15, 138, **177**
  mannerism in plays of, 75
  Measure for Measure, 15
  Midsummer Night's Dream, A, 216, **217**
  19th century revival of plays of, 133–34

  Othello, 138
  Richard II, **135**
  staging used by, 75, 77
  Taming of the Shrew, The, **74**
  Titus Andronicus, 77
  Two Gentlemen of Verona, The, 15
  Winter's Tale, A, 134, 136
  See also *Hamlet; Romeo and Juliet*
Sʜᴇᴘʜᴇʀᴅs ɪɴ ᴛʜᴇ Fɪᴇʟᴅs (royal portal of Chartres Cathedral), **62**
Sheridan, Richard Brinsley, 122. See also *The School for Scandal*
Siddons, Sarah, 120
Sɪʟᴇɴᴄᴇ (Redon), 168
Simonson, Lee, 173
Six Characters in Search of an Author (Pirandello), 140, 194, **202**
  analysis of, 199–200
  costumes for, 203
  lighting for, 203
  scenery and settings for, 200, **201**
Skene (Greek scene building), 32
Sᴏʟᴏᴍᴏɴ Rᴇᴄᴇɪᴠɪɴɢ ᴛʜᴇ Qᴜᴇᴇɴ ᴏꜰ Sʜᴇʙᴀ (Ghiberti), **8**
Sophocles, 37, 39, 40. See also *Oedipus Rex*
Stage effects. *See* Scenery and settings
Stanford Opera Theatre, production by, **23**
Stanford Players, productions by, 88, **202**
Stanford Repertory Theatre, productions by, **5,** 25, **26, 30, 31, 207, 209**
Stanford University, architecture of, 22, **24,** 25
Stanislavsky, Constantin, 153
  basic precepts of, 153
  production by, **152**
Sterling, Mrs., 81
Sᴛᴏɴᴇʙʀᴇᴀᴋᴇʀs, Tʜᴇ (Courbet), 149
Strindberg, August, 170

Index

"Stylized" productions, 21
Surrealism, 20
Swan Theatre, London, **76**
Symbolism, 20, 189
    in art, 147, 167–68, **169,** 170,
        171, 190
    expressionistic, 168, 170, **177,**
        184, 186, 188
    impressionistic, 168, 169, 170,
        178, **179, 181–82,** 183, 184
    in literature, 147, 163
    neomannerism as form of, 168,
        170, **171**
    in theatre, 168, 170, 173–87
        passim, **174–77, 179,**
        181–82, 188, 189, 199,
        211, 214
Sypher, Wylie, 15, 199

Tabor, Eron, **218**
Taming of the Shrew, The
    (Shakespeare), **74**
Tartuffe (Molière), 5, 6
    analysis of, 104, 123
    costumes for, **5,** 105, 107
    scenery and settings for, **5,**
        105, 107
Teatro Olimpico, Vincenza, 70, **71**
Tempietto, San Pietro in Montorio,
    Rome (Bramante), **12,** 13
Terence, 45, 47, 104
Theaters
    Baroque, 95, 97
    18th century, 116, 120, **121**
    Elizabethan, 70, 75, **76,** 77, 80, 85
    Greek, 32, **33**
    Italian Renaissance, 70, **71**
    19th century, 131, **132,** 133, 170

Roman, 45, 70
    20th century, 196, **197**
Théâtre du Vieux Colombier, Le
    (Paris), stage of, 196, **197**
Théâtre Libre, Paris, 150
Théâtre l'Oeuvre, Paris, 170
"Theatre of Cruelty," 216
There and Back (*Hin und Zurück*)
    (Hindemith; opera), **23**
THOUGHT, THE (Redon), 168
Tintoretto, 17, 69, 83, 88
    LAST SUPPER, THE, **69,** 86
Titus Andronicus (Shakespeare), **77**
Tom Payne, 216
Tragedy
    classical, in Baroque period,
        97, 99
    Greek, 31–32, 35, 37, 39–40, 43,
        45 (see also *Oedipus Rex;*
        Prometheus Bound)
Trash art, 205, **206**
Treasure of the Humble, The
    (Maeterlinck; essay), 180
Tribe, the, **218**
Turner, J. M. W., 129, 189
    RAIN, STEAM AND SPEED, **130**
Two Gentlemen of Verona, The
    (Shakespeare), 15
Tyrone Guthrie Theater. *See* Guthrie
    Theater, The

University of Kansas City,
    productions by, **101–2**

Valenciennes passion play, **56–57**
Vanbrugh, Sir John, 111
    Blenheim Palace, 111
    Relapse, The, 111, 112, **113**

Van Gogh, Vincent. *See* Gogh,
    Vincent van
Velásquez, Diego, 95
    CHRIST AND THE PILGRIMS OF
        EMMAUS, **96**
Vermeer, Jan, 103, 107
    A LADY AND GENTLEMAN AT THE
        VIRGINALS, **106**
Versailles, 108
Victorian fashion, in Renaissance
    plays, **2, 81,** 134, **136**
VIEW OF TOLEDO (El Greco), 10,
    11, 15
Vitruvius, 70
Voltaire, 120
Vos, Erik, production directed by,
    30, 31

Wagner, Richard, 170, 173
Wakefield cycle, 58. See also *The*
    Second Shepherd's Play
Walker, Nancy, **165**
Wasps, The (Aristophanes), 37
Watteau, Antoine, 115
    LES PLAISIRS DU BAL, **114**
Webb, John (Double-cubed Room
    at Wilton House), **109**
Winckelmann, Johann, 116
Winter's Tale, A (Shakespeare),
    134, **136**
Wölfflin, Heinrich, polarities set up
    by, 6, 8, 10, 13, 15
Wurzell, Stuart, sets by, **5**

Zeffirelli, Franco, 80
Zola, Émile, 150